GREAT GARDENS OF BRITAIN

ABOVE *Floribunda rose Copper-Pot; a child of Spek's Yellow, it flowers late into autumn.*

OVERLEAF *Bright sunshine in the garden at Pusey.*

GREAT GARDENS OF BRITAIN

PETER COATS

TREASURE
PRESS

First published in Great Britain by Artus Publishing Company Ltd

This edition published by Treasure Press
59 Grosvenor Street
London W1

© 1977 Peter Coats
Reprinted 1984

ISBN 0 907407 57 9

Printed in Hong Kong

ABOVE *Flora, in stone, in a rose-clad framework at Tyninghame.*

CONTENTS

LEFT *Massed spring blossom by the dove-cote at Nymans.*

BELOW *Tresco: set in a planting of rich foliage and flowers, a stone head of the god Neptune gazes out to sea.*

'What is it', it has often been asked, 'that makes the gardens of Britain the best in the world?' I have been asked that question many times and my answer is always the same – quality, diversity and . . . our climate.

Let us take quality first. The plan of a garden is composed of several different elements: lawns, hedges, borders, shrubberies, a greenhouse and a kitchen garden. It takes knowledge, skill, affection and patience to create any of these separate elements to perfection. The British excel at making and maintaining lawns – and the climate helps. Nowhere in the world are there lawns such as we have in Britain, and their lawns are one of the few things that the British are not tiresomely modest about. Hedges? We have the best hedges, too, because we know what to plant, other than privet or laurel; and clipping and tailoring hedges is a national passion. Our borders are better planned than any one sees abroad, and they are filled with a wider selection of plants. It is the same with our shrubberies, and there are more different shrubs and trees grown in our British gardens than in the whole of America. A garden can hardly be described as a garden if it has no greenhouse – how true is the saying 'Who loves a garden, loves a greenhouse too'. A British greenhouse may not intrinsically be better than an American or French one, but you may be sure that it will be stocked with more interesting plants, and a wider range of infant vegetables. So much for quality.

British gardeners garden in more different ways than those in other countries. In France, where there are the greatest gardens in the world, for we have nothing to compare with Versailles, there are really only two kinds of garden – the formal garden inspired, though sometimes on a tiny scale, by Versailles, or the *potager*: for the French love their vegetables, and though they may cook them better, they do not necessarily grow them better than we do. In Germany and Italy it is much the same – a few Baroque gardens of the greatest splendour but next to nothing on the manor house or rectory, let alone cottage, scale. In America the cypress gardens of the south are unique in their impressive beauty, but herbaceous borders, the well stocked shrubbery, the natural garden, or the streamside garden are very rare.

In Britain we have all these and more. We have the best herbaceous borders in the world – no doubt of that, if we only glance at the pictures in this book of the garden at Bampton Manor, Great Dixter, or at Nymans. We have the finest shrub gardens imaginable: Nymans again, or Bodnant, or Wakehurst. The topiary garden at Levens is probably the most impressive in the world, and for gardens of rare plants we need look no further than the extraordinary Tresco in the Scilly Isles.

For grandeur we may not be able to claim a garden equal to Versailles or Vaux le Vicomte, but the gardens at Powis Castle, at Chatsworth, or at Hampton Court are nothing to be ashamed of, and all three are without the slightly daunting quality of the giant lay-outs of Le Nôtre. And in all three of the 'grand' British gardens I have cited, the planting is of the greatest interest. The plants at Versailles or Vaux, though they may, in the mass, make an impressive blaze, are individually a common lot. Dusty Millers (Cineraria maritima) by the thousand, red salvias, white alyssum and blue lobelias are hardly plants of quality.

Lastly, our climate. We may complain about it incessantly, foreigners may joke about it, its vagaries may try us highly, but it does happen to be the best climate in the world for gardening. It is seldom too hot for too long – or too cold to do lasting damage. In a word, it is temperate.

Nearly all of the gardens I have chosen to include in this book are open to the public. They are scattered all over Britain, and for ease of reference have been grouped in different areas. In their quality and diversity they represent what I consider to be some of the best gardens we have. The location of each has been given, and the days and hours of opening, though these, of necessity, are sometimes changed: prospective visitors should check them before setting out on a long journey to see any particular garden.

At the end of this book details of three publications are given which are required reading for anyone who would like to know more about gardens in Britain to visit. Meanwhile, no better start could be made than to see at least a few of the thirty-three gardens I describe in the following pages. In my descriptions of each garden I have tried, wherever possible, to indicate to the prospective visitor what special feature of the garden he should look out for – old roses at Sissinghurst, garden architecture at Stourhead, and eucryphias at Nymans, for instance.

Rudyard Kipling, in one of his most famous poems, likened our whole country to a garden

> . . . that is full of stately views
> of borders, beds and shrubberies, and lawns and avenues
> With statues on the terraces and peacocks strutting by . . .

But he reminds us that

> . . . the glory of the garden lies in more than meets the eye.

Nowadays not many gardens boast peacocks (and they are very bad gardeners), but we have terraces still, though small ones, and even a statue or two. And the point Kipling makes about the garden's glory lying in more than meets the eye is as true now as on the day he made it. A garden is the product of years of work and dedication. Some of the gardens illustrated in this book are the result of the work of centuries. For even with the best gardening climate in the world, no garden can be made overnight.

Other peoples' gardens are ever fascinating. To visit them is to find not only inspiration but a kind of peace. Francis Bacon, in a famous essay, spoke truly when he wrote that a garden is 'the greatest refreshment for the spirits of man'.

PETER COATS

RIGHT *A corner of the Sunk Garden at Hampton Court in summer when the geraniums are in flower.*

1

THE HOME COUNTIES AND THE SOUTH

THE SAVILL GARDEN
Windsor, Berkshire

The Savill Garden in Windsor Great Park is certainly the largest and most important natural garden laid out and planted in this century. (It was first conceived fifty years ago). It owes its existence, mainly, to the foresight, imagination and perseverance of one man, Sir Eric Savill, at that time Deputy Ranger of Windsor Park. Sir Eric found a magnificent setting, with historic oaks and a romantic stretch of water, in which to lay out his garden. He was also fortunate in the continuing interest and enthusiasm of the royal family for the scheme. But the Savill Garden is in no way private or royal, for it is open throughout the year for the public to visit. It has become one of the great attractions for overseas visitors to Britain, and for gardeners from all over the world.

A natural garden, of which the Savill is such a good example, is, in the simplest terms, a garden planted in an area already well furnished with fine trees, where plants are set and then left to look after themselves. Rhododendrons in woodland, for example, or daffodils in grass under cherries.

The Savill Garden, now half a century old, contains as fine a collection of rhododendrons (the acid soil in the Windsor area suits them well), magnolias and camellias as anywhere in the country. Primulas and lilacs are another feature in spring. In June and July the rose garden is bright with colour, and one part is set aside for those popular shrubs of today, 'old fashioned' roses – those with such evocative names as 'Napoleon's Hat' and 'Thigh of a startled Nymph'.

Besides the Savill Garden proper, which centres on a beautiful stretch of water, there is also the Valley Garden, where some of the rarest, tallest rhododendrons are to be admired. This is much larger (nearly 200 acres) and extends almost to Virginia Water; it is a later creation.

To the south-east lies the Kurume Punchbowl, a spacious natural amphitheatre which has been planted with sheets of azaleas in groups of different colours. For many weeks in summer the Punchbowl presents one of the most spectacular shows of colour in the world.

There is almost no time in the year when there is not something to see in the Savill Garden and the gardens adjacent to it. In spring the waterside is starred with primulas, as well as with our own native primroses and bluebells, which always seem to spring up by magic when trees are thinned. The rhododendrons follow, some of which may have been in flower since Christmas. In June and July, the herbaceous borders, all of 35 feet wide, blaze from end to end: these are of note to the gardener as they are planted not only with herbaceous material, which dies down in winter, but with some evergreen and silver-leaved shrubs to give form and some colour even in December.

LEFT *Old trees of Windsor Great Park by the lake.*

BELOW *'A natural garden . . . is a garden planted in an area already well furnished with fine trees.'*

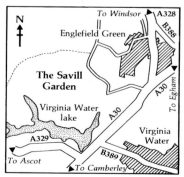

An interesting and touching corner of the gardens is the area sheltered by a wall built from the bricks of London buildings destroyed in the blitz. Here grow many rare and tender plants which would hardly thrive in the open. Of this very special area of the Savill Garden it has been said, by the well known American garden expert, Lanning Roper, 'Here beauty and life have become the by-products of destruction and death.'

OPEN March 1st–October 31st: daily. 10 a.m.–6 p.m.
Valley Gardens open all year.
LOCATION Signposted from Ascot, Englefield Green, Windsor and Egham.

RIGHT *Lush and varied foliage by the border of the lake.*

BELOW *In the spring azalea mollis fills the air around with scent.*

STEARTHILL
Buckinghamshire

The garden at Stearthill is open to the public all summer through and well repays a visit. It was planned and first planted by Colonel and Mrs Close-Smith, but since becoming a widow Mrs Close-Smith has done much to develop and add to the garden and generally imbue it with her own taste.

Stearthill Garden is of special interest to the average garden visitor. Far from large, it is big enough to have a dozen unexpected corners to fascinate and please the visitor. When Mrs Close-Smith first decided to open it to the public she was afraid it might be too small, or too simple.

Far from being too small, I discovered that most people, particularly coach parties on an afternoon's outing, thought it just right; not too far to walk, with plenty of seats – and the coach could back right up to the tea-room. Others inspected the lawns and edges and complimented me on their tidiness. The first summer I opened was a fine one; everyone was enthusiastic and anxious to tell me they had enjoyed themselves . . . to such an extent I was almost ashamed to take their money. It pleased me to think that the garden itself had heard the compliments flying about. There was also great satisfaction in knowing that with only a minimum amount of help to do the heavy work, every tree, shrub and plant had been planted with one's own hands.

If, for some overwhelming economic reason, the garden had to be bulldozed back to rough grass, I know a part of me would die with it; but I hope this will not happen and that the garden will continue to give pleasure to a lot of people besides myself.

Judging by the crowds that find their way to Stearthill every summer, it seems that such fears are groundless. It is a garden well worth visiting, and, for rose lovers, worth visiting year after year because, like all good gardeners, Mrs Close-Smith can be hard-hearted as well as sentimental, and if a rose fails or disappoints, out it comes to be replaced by a different rose.

Roses have been a passion of Mrs Close-Smith's ever since, twenty-two years ago, she read a book on old shrub roses and was completely carried away: so much so that she at once determined to possess a collection of old roses second only to the one created by the Empress Josephine at Malmaison – quite an ambition. But that was not the only reason she decided to concentrate on roses. Contributing factors were the prevailing wind, and the unyielding clay soil. It was, and is, totally unsiftable; a bog in wet weather; like concrete in dry: in short, the most back-aching and uncompromising stuff to deal with. But she knew that roses would put up with it better than most plants. So roses it was.

However, a rose garden is hard work. It must always be immaculate. Every week it must be mown and edged up and dead-headed, and hoed when

Massed flowers of Hybrid Tea roses by the terrace. Stella, pink and cream Helen Traubel, apricot and Spek's Yellow are three favourites. In the foreground Arthur Bell.

17

necessary. At least once a month, from April until the end of the flowering season, it must be sprayed against greenfly, caterpillar, mildew and black spot, in that order. In the winter pruning is a long, exacting and painful job; and someone has to climb to the top of the wall to tie in the roses against it.

These are some of the many hundreds of roses which the visitor to Stearthill will find, and the purposes they fulfil. For colour and effect early in the season: cantabrigiensis and ecae, both with yellow flowers and growing into erect feathery bushes. All the Frühlings group, though they need plenty of space. Frühlingsanfang (cream), Frühlingsduft (double buff) and Frühlingsgold (yellow) are all splendid in bloom.

The single cream Nevada and the hybrid pink Marguerite Hilling are also good flowerers, and flower simultaneously. A much lower growing group, the spinosissimas, of which Altaica (white), William III (dark red) and Falkland (double pale pink) are very useful. All the foregoing are sweetly scented, but they only flower once.

Next in the garden at Stearthill come the rugosas, China and musk roses. The rugosas are mostly self-supporting, about 5 to 6 feet high and wide, sweet-smelling and twice-flowering. The single varieties produce huge scarlet tomato-shaped hips and their foliage turns brilliant yellow in the autumn. They are resistant to all forms of disease, mildew and blackspot. What more could one ask?

The musks are equally sturdy, but more delicate in flower and scent, though not so resistant to disease. Most are about 4 to 5 feet high and wide, and when out they make a solid mass of colour. Penelope (cream with apricot shadings), Felicia (clear pink), Buff Beauty and Cornelia (pink), are the best. The lesser

RIGHT *Canna lilies by the indoor swimming pool.*

BELOW *In June roses cover the walls of the garden with a curtain of flower.*

known Daybreak, Autumn Delight (both cream), Thisbe (yellow), and the cool white Moonlight with its handsome bronze foliage, are four other good varieties.

Of the summer flowering species roses for mixing amongst shrubs, rubrifolia is a beauty with its purple-red leaves. The Moyesii and multibracteata varieties are thorny but very effective and multibracteata Cerise Bouquet has an amazingly long flowering period. There are also some large hybrid-modern shrub roses such as Scarlet Fire, Poulsen's Pink Park, Zitronenfalter and Sparrieshoop.

As to hybrid teas, Fragrant Cloud and its stablemate, Prima Ballerina, rank very high. Piccadilly is a superb and strong orange-yellow bicolor with rich bronze young foliage. Stella, equally good, is pink and cream. Helen Traubel (apricot with blue-grey foliage), is an old favourite, and Spek's Yellow still takes a lot of beating as a bedding rose.

For floribundas, Arthur Bell (double yellow), and two new-comers, Southampton (apricot), and Escapade (single mauve), do well at Stearthill, while Elizabeth of Glamis has been found to be the best salmon pink, 'and I could not do without Iceberg'.

Trees and shrubs, other than roses, which create a good contrast in the borders at Stearthill are sea buckthorn, tamarisk, purple nut, all the deutzias,

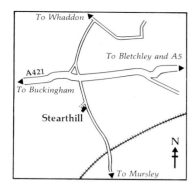

spring and summer flowering hebes, mahonias and hydrangeas. For the front of the border there are potentillas, hostas and species geraniums the best of which are armenum, Renardii, ibericum and Endressii; all indispensable for weed suppression. The dogwood Cornus elegantissima with variegated green and white leaves, and Eleagnus aurea with green and yellow variegation are splendid mixers. The spring flowering herbaceous paeonies Mlokosewitschii (sulphur yellow) and obovata alba (white) are also great favourites, underplanted with Viola labradorica.

The visitor to Stearthill should not miss the really old and romantic varieties of roses, such as the historic Red Rose of Lancaster, the White Rose of York, Rosa mundi – so often called the York and Lancaster, but reputedly named after Henry II's 'Fair Rosamond' – Rosa frankofurtana, previously called 'Empress Josephine', and the crested Chapeau de Napoleon. Bloomfield Abundance and mutabilis are two very good old China Roses and Perle d'Or is a little beauty with buttonhole apricot blooms. If planted with tree lupins and musk rose Buff Beauty, they provide flowers for months on end.

Before the visitor leaves this interesting garden, the indoor swimming pool must be inspected. Around it grow a dozen rarities such as canna lilies, abutilons and tender begonias, and a banana palm which would not survive an instant in the keen Buckinghamshire breezes.

But it is not for such exotics that the garden is noted, it is for its roses, and from May until October the garden at Stearthill is a place of scented enchantment, with roses, roses all the way.

NOTE: Stearthill House and garden have recently changed hands and the garden is not at the moment open to the public.

LEFT *Tender plants, such as sweet geraniums and delicate fuchsias, thrive in the glass-walled garden room.*

BELOW RIGHT *In July the large flowered clematis such as white Miss Bateman come into their own.*

BELOW *A tapestry of roses.*

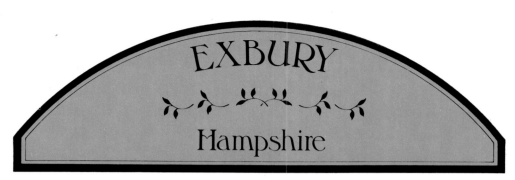

EXBURY
Hampshire

If any one garden in Britain is synonymous with a single plant, Exbury must surely be synonymous with azaleas. The Exbury strain of azalea has spread the fame of the Hampshire garden all over the world. And, of course, Exbury is not only celebrated for this shrub, but for the kindred family of rhododendrons as well.

The garden at Exbury is not old. In fact it was only fifty-five years ago that the late Mr Lionel Rothschild started raising azaleas and rhododendrons in earnest. Oddly enough, the soil at Exbury is poor, but the gravelly loam of which it is composed happens to be the perfect soil for the plants for which this garden has become so well known. Roses do not do well at Exbury, nor do lilacs; lime-loving plants such as viburnums are hardly worth planting; but rhododendrons and azaleas are happy there, and in early spring and summer the garden is one of the sights of southern England. The maritime climate, too, is kind, and the temperature at Exbury is often several degrees higher than that found only a few miles inland. Frosts are comparatively rare.

Rhododendrons found their way into British gardens following the discovery of a plant of Rhododendron ponticum growing in the wild, in Spain. The botanist who discovered the plant was a Swede, Baron Alstroemer, the date shortly before 1763. Alstroemer was a friend of the celebrated horticulturist, Carl Linnaeus, originator of the nomenclature of plants, who gave his friend's name to the well known alstroemeria.

By 1763 R. ponticum was well established in the British colony of Gibraltar, and its famous, or infamous, career had begun. R. ponticum needs no description. Over parts of England and Scotland it has become almost a weed. But it has great qualities, and it is invaluable as a stock plant on which to graft many varieties and species which do not root readily from cuttings, or are difficult to layer.

But the garden visitor does not come to Exbury in search of Rhododendron ponticum. Under the green canopy of the ancient cedars, trees two hundred years older than the garden they shade, are to be found the rarest species of rhododendrons. Plants such as the great Sino-grande from the uplands of China – R. falconeri, with leaves that are underfelted with tan-coloured fur; R. campylocarpum from the Himalayas; the blue-flowered R. Augustinii; the red-flowered R. arboreum from the hillsides of Ceylon; the round-leaved orbiculare; and a rhododendron which is found in very few gardens, the Tibetan R. concatenans, which has leaves scented like incense. That is to name just a few.

Many famous new hybrid rhododendrons have been raised at Exbury, and from two strains in particular, RR. campylocarpum and discolor. These were

Azaleas when in full flower show hardly a leaf.
The Exbury strains are known all over the world.

introduced into England at the turn of the century, and soon after Mr Rothschild started breeding rhododendrons professionally, 'a marriage was arranged' between these two great plants, from which many distinguished descendants have resulted. R. campylocarpum transmits its yellow flowers to many of its descendants, while R. discolor transmits its attractive grey-green leaves and lavishness of flower. One of the results of this 'marriage' was a rhododendron which Mr Lionel de Rothschild named after a friend, Lady Bessborough. This beautiful new plant first flowered in 1933 and was, in due course, crossed with another rhododendron, the yellow flowered R. Wardii (named after one of the last and greatest of all plant collectors, Captain F. Kingdon-Ward). From this cross descended the first of the impressive Hawk hybrids, which are some of the best yellow-flowered rhododendrons in cultivation.

Another famous rhododendron first raised at Exbury is an exquisite flowerer, Lady Chamberlain. This was called after another personal friend of the Rothschilds, the wife of Sir Austen Chamberlain. It is a really beautiful plant, and is the offspring of the glaucous-leaved R. cinnabarinum roylei (first discovered in Sikkum by Sir Joseph Hooker) and Royal Flush. It is from Royal Flush that Lady Chamberlain inherits its distinctive apricot-coloured flowers.

A few more remain to be acclaimed, especially some of the named varieties of rhododendrons with unusual pastel-coloured flowers, plants such as Elizabeth de Rothschild, Repose and Halcyon, and the Jalisco group which

ABOVE *Rhododendron macabeanum has yellow flowers and enormous leaves.*

BELOW *A cedar tree . . . 'two hundred years older than the garden it shades'.*

offers flowers in stronger shades. Rouge, Nicholas and Nehru are further out-standing Exbury introductions.

But the strain of plants raised by Mr Lionel de Rothschild which has made the name of the garden at Exbury resound in the world of horticulture is the Exbury strain of azaleas. The parent plants of these were the ordinary Ghent azalea and the brilliant orange-coloured A. calendulaceum, the 'sky paint flower' of the Cherokees. The grandparents were A. occidentale (from which the Exbury strains of azalea inherit their strong scent) and A. arborescens. The Exbury strains are at their best in May and June, and with their heady perfume, their graceful spreading habit of growth and large, well-formed flowers, are among the most beautiful and most useful shrubs of early summer.

Lionel de Rothschild died in 1942, in the middle of the war – a difficult time for gardening. The house at Exbury had been requisitioned by the Admiralty, and its widespread plantations of precious shrubs, like all gardens in wartime, had to suffer neglect. Many of the finest plants were strangled by nettles and brambles and yet, today, thirty-five years after, so vigorously do rhododen-drons and azaleas grow in the gentle climate of that part of Hampshire, that any spaces have long been filled up, and some thinning out is necessary every year.

From early spring onwards the garden at Exbury is a scene of enchantment. Perhaps it is at its peak in early March when the splendid rhododendron Red Admiral is in full flower; or perhaps in April, when the blue Rhododendron

There are rhododendrons at Exbury from China, Tibet and the Himalayas.

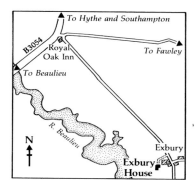

augustinii and yellow R. campylocarpum are at their best. These grow in broad swathes under the tall Scots pines, and there are daffodils everywhere to contrast with, or echo, the lucent colour of their flowers.

In May Exbury's own azaleas come into bloom and edge one side of the lake with colour, their brilliance set off by the bright green of Griselinia littoralis. In the middle of the lake is an island, upon which grows a fine specimen of Taxodium distichum, the swamp cypress of the southern United States, a tree which loves to have its feet in water and thrives in just that situation.

Visitors who have visited Exbury in the past will surely remember Fred Wynniatt, head gardener there for many years. Recently a part of the garden by the middle pond has been christened the Wynniatt Bowl and planted with evergreen azaleas in memory of that great gardener and dedicated plantsman.

Among the fine specimens of trees and shrubs at Exbury, other than rhododendrons, are some interesting, seldom-grown oaks, such as the Hungarian oak (Quercus frainetto) which will thrive on almost any soil including chalk, and Quercus canariensis with its dark grey, deeply fissured bark and glossy green leaves. These two splendid trees have been described as even superior in rate of growth to our own native species. Another very special tree to be seen at Exbury is Magnolia veitchii which shows its beautiful white flowers, flushed with purple, on its leafless branches in April. Two other trees worth noting are Fagus sylvatica latifolia, our native beech, but one with leaves far larger than the type; and the Manna Ash (Fraxinus ornus), covered with flowers in May.

LEFT *The garden at Exbury is famous for rhododendrons.*

BELOW *Lysichitum americanum, a kind of arum, loves to grow by water. Though a handsome plant it has an unpleasant smell – hence its popular name, Skunk Cabbage.*

Some distinguished conifers to be seen in this remarkable garden are the Serbian spruce (Picea Omorica), which quickly makes a tall, graceful tree; a cypress (Cupressus arizonica) of columnar habit and rich green foliage; and the fabled redwood from California (Sequoia sempervirens). This, on its native heath, reaches the almost incredible height of 366 feet. The highest redwood recorded in Britain lags far behind that sky-scraping record, but has been measured and found to be (in 1970) all of 138 feet high. It is in a garden in north Devon.

Two last conifers at Exbury must be mentioned. Fitzroya cupressoides, introduced by William Lobb from South America in 1851, and the Californian Nutmeg (Torreya californica), another Lobb introduction. This is a handsome, broadly conical tree which, with its medium size, would grace any garden, large or comparatively small. It was called after Dr John Torrey, a distinguished American botanist of the last century.

But for the amateur garden visitor to Exbury, perhaps the most heart warming impression will be made by the rosy-pink candle flowers of the rare Magnolia campbellii, the giant Himalayan 'pink tulip tree'. Though this is a tree for the patient gardener as it seldom flowers before its twenty-fifth year, an established specimen, in full flower in February, is a memorable sight. There are two such splendid magnolias at Exbury, and they are worth going a very long way to see.

OPEN First Sunday in April – mid June: daily, including weekends, 2 p.m. – 6.30 p.m.
LOCATION Between Beaulieu and Lymington. Leave B3054 at Royal Oak Inn, signposted from there.

HEVER CASTLE
Kent

'Four hundred years ago', it has been written, 'the beam of history was fixed on Hever Castle ... it was to illuminate the place with a hectic glory for several years, a light which faded to a baleful glow and finally – and disastrously – disappeared. The sunlit peace which envelopes Hever Castle and its gardens today is in startling contrast.'

The historical background to the gardens at Hever is of such interest that it must be outlined before any detailed description of them is undertaken. The Castle, in the sixteenth century, was the home of the Boleyns, a worldly ambitious family whose social aspirations were, literally, crowned, when the daughter of the house, Anne, achieved marriage with King Henry VIII. After Anne's execution the fortunes of the Boleyns – and of their home – declined. In the first years of the present century, the Castle itself was lived in by a farmer. The proud banqueting hall had become a kitchen, hung with hams. Sacks of corn and potatoes were stacked in upper chambers that were haunted with memories of royal lovemaking.

. Then in 1903 an American, and a great lover of Britain and its gardens, saw the little moated castle, fell in love with it, and set about its restoration. The development of the gardens was spectacular: the course of the River Eden was changed; public roads were moved further away, and out of sight, a 35-acre lake was conjured in some of the low-lying meadows which lay around. To beautify his new pleasure grounds Mr Astor transported fully-grown trees from Ashdown Forest, a specialized art in which Americans have always excelled, and rocks were moved in to edge the lake and form a cascade. All this was done on a scale unseen in England since Joseph Paxton moved the great rocks at Chatsworth (described elsewhere in this book), causing his patron to say that the 'spirit of a Druid inspires Mr Paxton in these bulky removals'.

A totally new landscape was conjured round the castle itself, where a series of new gardens sprang into being. To the west, 'Anne Boleyn's Orchard' was set out and thousands of daffodils were planted to lay a golden carpet every spring. In 1906 another area was planned, and dedicated to King Henry's luckless queen. This lies to the east of the Castle, and comprises that favourite device of the Tudors, a maze. Nearby, and framed in perfectly clipped yew, are glowing beds of scarlet tulips and red Frensham roses. An interesting centre-piece in this part of the 'new' garden (though it is already seventy years of age) is a gilded astrolabe, which the present owner, Lord Astor of Hever, describes in his careful notes on the garden, as an 'old astronomical instrument for measuring the altitude of celestial bodies, from which it is possible to estimate, roughly, time and latitude'.

RIGHT *An astrolabe, a device formerly used in the study of the stars, in one of the smaller, yew-walled gardens at Hever.*

BELOW *William Waldorf Astor collected many fine bits of antique Roman sculpture to adorn his English garden.*

ABOVE *Light and shade: scattered topiary trees in the garden at Hever.*

ABOVE LEFT *Tulips growing in long grass brighten the scene in early summer.*

BELOW LEFT *The lily-strewn moat.*

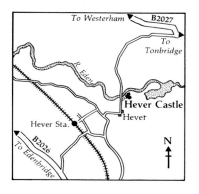

As Tudor in feeling as the Maze is the nearby Herb Garden, set out with all the herbs beloved of cooks of long ago (and of discerning ones of today) such as sage, thyme, mint and golden marjoram – aromatic plants with spicy leaves that keep their 'seeming and savour all the winter long'.

Not far away from the Herb Garden lies a garden with happier associations than those connected with unfortunate Anne Boleyn. This is the Silver Garden, laid out in October 1970 to commemorate Lord and Lady Astor's Silver Wedding. Here are to be found all the various plants of grey and argent foliage which are so popular with modern garden planners: artemisia, santolina, stachys, anaphalis, and a dozen others. Many of them keep their lucent leaves all the year round and so add a welcome glint and glitter to the garden, even in winter.

The gardens at Hever are many and varied. The Rhododendron Walk is in full beauty in early summer, with the scented Loders White, and the pink budded King George as its star attractions. Recently Mr Astor's original Golden Stairs and Quarry Garden were cleared and planted anew with shade-loving plants such as hostas, astilbes and Kurume azaleas, with, where there is a patch of sunlight, yellow brooms and hypericums to give their individual touches of gold.

By far the most unusual feature of the gardens at Hever is the Italian Garden. Here are collected the classical statuary and sculpture which Mr Astor amassed while American Ambassador in Rome. But, being a man of taste and tact, he was careful to place his collection of sculptures so that it could not be seen from the Tudor Castle, with which it might have looked out of place. The Italian Garden is approached by crossing the outer moat and following a wide path with lawn on either side. The statuary, Corinthian columns, sarcophagi and marble gods and goddesses are placed under a long wall of old stone; this is an eighth of a mile long, and richly clothed, for all its length, with roses, magnolias and vines. It is the inspired juxtaposition of foliage and flower with stonework and marble which makes the success of this very special part of the garden at Hever. Marble, under grey English skies, can look cold and forbidding: it needs flowers and the trailing leaves of climbing plants to set it off, and soften the effect.

The gardens at Hever Castle, with their variety, their historical associations and their beautiful setting, present as fair a prospect as any in Britain. Within easy reach of London, they should come very high on any list of gardens that must be visited.

OPEN First Sunday in April – end of September: Wednesday, Sunday and Bank Holidays, 1 p.m. – 7 p.m.
LOCATION Signposted from Edenbridge.

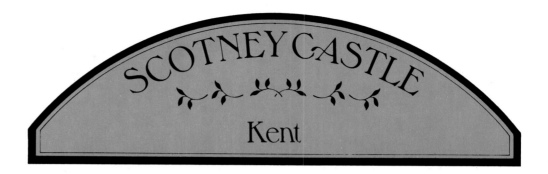

SCOTNEY CASTLE
Kent

The garden at Scotney Castle is in a setting which must surely be one of the most unusual and spectacular in the country. In an unfrequented valley, its sides clothed with ancient trees, lies a little lake. In the middle of the lake, or moat, is a ruined castle (though it is a carefully and lovingly preserved ruin) around which the garden was planned and over two centuries has grown to maturity.

The Old Castle was built in 1378, in the reign of the unfortunate Richard II, by Roger de Ashburnham. Its structure and architectural detail show a remarkable resemblance to those of another famous Sussex castle, Bodiam, built ten years later. Old Scotney Castle was never meant to be a fortress: it was intended to be more of a fortified house. A detailed history of the Castle, and its occupants, is admirably set out in the official guide book which was written by that great expert of English houses and castles, the late Christopher Hussey, whose family has lived at Scotney since 1778.

Early in the last century the Mrs Hussey of the day decided that the Castle was damp and unhealthy, which in those days without central heating it almost certainly was. She took herself and her young son off to salubrious St Leonards. This son, Christopher Hussey's grandfather, was a keen amateur architect, and it was he who, when he came of age, decided to demolish the old family home, though preserving it as a picturesque ruin, and to build a new house nearby on higher, healthier ground.

The style he chose for his new house was a restrained Victorian Tudor, the material he selected was the ironstone from his own quarry in the new part of the garden, and the architect he appointed was Anthony Salvin, already a leading expert on the revival of Tudor architecture for country houses. The new house was completed in 1843, and owes much of its pleasing appearance to Edward Hussey's inspired use of the beautifully textured and coloured local stone.

The Old Castle [writes Christopher Hussey], though the Tudor portion continued to be inhabited by the estate bailiff till 1905, was thenceforth regarded as an historic and picturesque object in connection with the garden landscape. In other circumstances, it might well have been demolished or left to fall down. Instead part of the seventeenth century range was carefully taken down in such a way as to retain features of interest and increase the romantic character of the scene, and cause the mediaeval and Tudor portion to predominate. So originated the conception of treating the Old Castle and adjoining hillsides in the way that an artist composes a painting – but with vegetation, water and masonry instead of pigments.

LEFT *Old Scotney Castle, a carefully preserved, romantic ruin, lies at the bottom of a steep slope, clothed every spring with flowering shrubs.*

BELOW *Blue flowered ceanothus and Magnolia grandiflora clothe one of the walls of the new Scotney Castle, built during the short reign of William IV (1830–37).*

This brings us to the garden. The most spectacular view of the garden at Scotney is from the semi-circular balustraded bastion, built high above the quarry from which the stone for the new house was originally obtained. Under a high canopy of age-old beeches, banks of smaller flowering trees and shrubs cover the steep slope which falls towards the Old Castle in its lily-strewn moat.

Some of the shrubs are of great interest, though the garden at Scotney, unlike some of the gardens described in this book, is not a garden of exotic plants or rarities. Indeed, in such a supremely English setting they might look tawdry and out of place: out of period, certainly.

Two particular plantings deserve mention. First, the largest group of calico bushes (Kalmia latifolia) from eastern North America which the author of this book has ever seen. These make a brave show when they are their full, pink bloom in June. Second are the splendid groups, round the water's edge, of the royal fern, (Osmunda regalis). This plant is said to get its curious name Osmunda from that of a Saxon Princess whose father hid her in a clump of the fern to hide her from the attentions of the invading Danes. The Old Castle's walls are hung with roses, pink, white and mauve in summer, and nearby there is a new herb garden which seems in perfect keeping with its ancient setting.

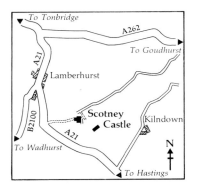

With roses on its crumbling walls and a moat starred with water lilies, the old castle makes a beautiful picture in summer.

RIGHT *The old and the new: massed narcissus under ancient trees.*

But it is not to admire individual flowers or borders that visitors seek out Scotney. It is for the unforgettable view of the old Castle, in its moat, from Edward Hussey's bastion; it is to admire the masterly placing of the trees – an incense cedar (Libocedrus decurrens) in contrast with the horizontal growth of a cedar of Lebanon; and above all it is to experience the deep peace, and sense of time standing still, which pervades the whole domain.

The Hussey family motto, inscribed under the coat of arms on the porch, is '*Vix ea nostra voco*' ('I scarcely call these things our own'). Though Mrs Christopher Hussey still lives at Scotney and takes an active interest in the garden, this is now the charge of the National Trust, so the wording of the motto has in part come true. It is a happy solution. For Mrs Hussey herself, to see the garden so well looked after, and so widely appreciated; and for visitors, who have a chance of coming to spend an hour or two, under a very special spell.

OPEN April – end of October: daily except Monday and Tuesday. Open Bank Holidays. April – October: 2 p.m. – 5 p.m. May – September: 2 p.m. – 6 p.m.
LOCATION $\frac{1}{2}$ mile south of Lamberhurst on A21 London to Hastings road.

35

SISSINGHURST CASTLE
Kent

The gardens at Sissinghurst Castle have been described as the most beautiful in England. They were created, in the romantic setting of the ruined Castle walls, in the last half-century, by two brilliant amateur gardeners, Sir Harold Nicolson and his wife, the poet Victoria Sackville-West.

Sissinghurst Castle itself dates from the reign of Henry VIII, and has had a varied history. Horace Walpole described it in 1752 as 'perfect and very beautiful' – but eight years later it was being used as a gaol for French prisoners-of-war. Soon after, most of the building had become ruined, except for the dominating tower.

The Nicolsons bought Sissinghurst in 1930, and at once set about creating the garden that the visitor sees today. What makes the garden so special is the architectural way in which it has been planned, the surviving walls of rosy old brick and newly planted hedges of yew and beech, making a crisp and scholarly framework for the brimming flowerbeds. Today, fifty years later, the hedges have grown to maturity, and look as if they might have been there in Tudor times. The walls are hung with roses, vines and unusual climbing plants; each enclosed part of the garden has its own character and appeal; each border its own carefully devised colour scheme.

LEFT *Daffodils by the little garden house built in memory of the creators of the garden.*

ABOVE *The outline of the Tudor castle tower is*
echoed by a slim evergreen. All around lies
the garden, one of the most famous in Britain.

The original plan for the garden was not an easy one to make. There were no old trees, as might have been expected, to act as focal points. The courtyard, or what was left of it, was not square with the tower. But with thought and ingenuity, all the existing features were woven into an overall scheme, which today can be seen to be totally successful.

What are the main features of the garden at Sissinghurst? The tower, of course, soaring aloft over the multi-coloured carpet of gardens which lie at its feet. The two rondels, an old word revived by Victoria Sackville-West, who vividly recalls the 'stab of pleasure' when she discovered that that was the word the local Kentish people gave to the circular area surrounded by a hedge, where they used to dry hops. The rondels at Sissinghurst are turfed and left free of planting. With their green lawns and circular walls of dark yew, they offer areas of quiet and rest for eyes which might otherwise have become almost sated with all the colour round about.

ABOVE *In a corner of the cottage garden orange lilies and golden solidago and montbretia make a rich picture.*

RIGHT *The South Cottage garden is planted in warm colours of red, bronze, orange and yellow. It was in the cottage that Sir Harold Nicolson used to write.*

ABOVE LEFT *A view of the garden from the tower, showing the sharply-cut pattern of the garden and one of the rondels.*

RIGHT *Massed polyanthus revel in the light shade of the 'Nuttery'.*

LEFT *The Herb Garden – with paved paths and a flat stone vase, planted with red-leaved sempervivum, as a centre-piece. Sempervivum, or house leeks, are said to ward off evil spirits.*

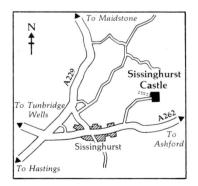

Colour plays a great part in the planting at Sissinghurst, and it is colour which gives the garden its unique character. There are blue borders, borders devised in tones of claret, rose and silver, a small garden-within-a-garden which is daringly planted in shades of orange, yellow and bronze. Most spectacular is the White Garden which presents, when at its height, a dreamy bridal chamber for a statue of a young girl. The White Garden has been acclaimed as the most beautiful of all the clustered gardens at Sissinghurst and is at its best in June 'when cloudy with white roses growing through almond trees . . . its air laden with the incense of white regale lilies . . . their flowers afloat, it seems, on a mist of gypsophila and silver-leaved plants'.

The creators of the garden are both dead, but the garden is beautifully maintained by the National Trust and is always open in the summer. But each year, it seems, the observant visitor seems to notice little differences. One planting scheme is richer, a new brick path has been added, a shrub which, as the Kentish say 'has come too mighty', has been tactfully cut back. For no garden must remain static and the most perfect of parterres can be improved. Much love and thought – and back-breaking work – goes into the maintenance of the high standard of the garden at Sissinghurst. Few visitors, and certainly no garden enthusiast, can leave it without a lifting of the heart.

OPEN April 1st – October 15th: daily. Monday – Friday: 12 a.m. – 6.30 p.m. Saturday, Sunday and Bank Holidays: 10 a.m. – 6.30 p.m. LOCATION 1 mile north-east of Sissinghurst village on A262. 16 miles south of Maidstone.

The border below the red brick wall is
full of colour from spring onwards.

HAMPTON COURT
Middlesex

The Garden at Hampton Court, with the possible exception of Chatsworth, described elsewhere in this book, is the grandest in England. It owes its present form to King William III and his wife, Queen Mary, who had passed their early married life in Holland, and were much influenced by the continental style of gardening then prevalent. Perhaps Dutch William dreamed, once he became king of England in 1688, of having a garden to rival that of his enemy, Louis XIV, at Versailles. If so, he never achieved it, though he made a brave attempt. The temperature – political rather than climatic – in England does not favour too grandiose conceptions on the part of her kings. Hampton Court is but a modest echo of Versailles, but echo it is, and an impressive one.

Hampton Court, as everyone knows, was built by Cardinal Wolsey and given by him, with some ill grace, to Henry VIII; and it is of the garden in Henry VIII's time that we first have records. We know that he laid out bowling greens, built a tennis court (it still exists) and archery butts. He planted a rose garden to supply roses for his current wife, Anne Boleyn, especially, and threw up the fashionable mound, with a glass-paned summer house on top. The most striking part of the garden in Tudor times was a *parterre* embellished not only with flowers, but with high poles painted white and green, the Tudor colours. On top of these poles were garishly coloured carved figures of the 'King's Beastes', a series of heraldic animals such as the Black Bull of Clarence, the Griffon of Edward III and that strange animal, the horned and walrus-toothed Yale of Beaufort.

All the Tudors loved their palace on the river Thames. So did the succeeding Stuarts. Charles II wanted to emulate the gardens he had seen on the continent in his days of exile, but never had the money to complete his ambitious schemes. However, he had the still-existing canal dug, and planted the lime avenues which still radiate from the palace: during his reign, the gardens must have presented a gay appearance, with ladies and gentlemen such as Lely painted walking in it, and enjoying to the full, as the visiting Duke of Tuscany disapprovingly recorded, 'snug places of retirement, in certain towers'.

James II's reign was short, and saw little change at Hampton Court. It was not until the Glorious Revolution of 1688 that the gardens took the form in which we see them today. William and Mary, with the aid of Sir Christopher Wren, not only transformed Wolsey's palace, but made great alterations to the garden. The Maze was planted, the Long and Broad Walks were laid out, and the Great Fountain Garden was designed below the east facade of the palace: to make room for this, some of Charles II's canal had to be filled in. The Great Fountain Garden, still one of the most spectacular parts of the pleasure grounds at Hampton Court, owes much to King William's native Holland, and something to France, with its *broderie* of box trees in an almost Baroque design of flowerbeds set with hyacinths or tulips, or relying for colour on powdered brick – *brique pilée*, such as Le Nôtre used for his stupendous creation at Versailles.

Two famous names now take their place in the story of the garden at Hampton Court, Daniel Marot and Jean Tijou. Marot certainly had a hand in the design of some of King William's parterres, and Tijou made the drawings for the twelve beautiful grilles, which still grace the garden: two in their original position in the Great Fountain Garden, and the others in the Privy Garden.

Only the renewed outbreak of war with France prevented further changes. As it was, the last vestiges of the Tudor garden were swept away, including Henry VIII's tilt yard and famous mound.

Queen Anne came often to Hampton Court. As the smell of box made her sneeze, much of William's parterre was uprooted. But Anne's association with Hampton Court has been caught for us in an amber moment by Alexander Pope in the opening lines of *The Rape of the Lock*:

> *Close by those Meads for ever crown'd with Flow'rs*
> *Where Thames with Pride surveys his rising Tow'rs*
> *There stands a Structure of Majestic Fame,*
> *Which from the neighb'ring Hampton takes its name.*
> *Here thou, great Anna! whom three realms obey,*
> *Dost sometimes Counsel take – and sometimes Tea*

Tea, in those days, being pronounced 'Tay'.

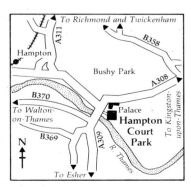

ABOVE *Knot-gardens were a tradition in Tudor days. There is a modern version at Hampton Court, complete with intricate, interlacing hedges of box, lavender and santolina, and neatly gravelled paths.*

ABOVE LEFT *The Great Vine, one of the sights of the garden for over two hundred years.*

LEFT *Hampton Court, of which the later part was built for William III in the last years of the seventeenth century by Sir Christopher Wren (1632–1723).*

George II engaged both William Kent and Charles Bridgeman to do some work at Hampton Court, and under their sway more of the formal gardens were swept away in deference to the fashion of the day for natural gardening, or, as it was called on the continent, *le jardin anglais*. Under George III the famous Lancelot 'Capability' Brown laid his hands on the place, but though a dedicated advocate of the natural style, he spared much of what was left of the formal gardens. It was he who planted the Great Vine which today is one of the wonders of Hampton Court.

George III's granddaughter, Queen Victoria, made the last and most sensational move in the history of the garden. She opened it to the public. This was a most unusual thing to do at that time, and in the first year 120,000 people thronged to see it.

Modern additions to the garden are splendid plantings of tulips in spring, followed in summer by a blaze of colour provided by two of the most spectacular herbaceous borders in the country; and a new knot garden re-echoes, after four centuries, the original Tudor flavour of Wolsey's palace.

OPEN November – February: 9.30 a.m. – 4 p.m. (Monday, Saturday, Sunday: 2 p.m. – 4 p.m.). March, April, October: 9.30 a.m. – 5 p.m. (Sunday: 2 p.m. – 4 p.m.). May – September: 9.30 a.m. – 6 p.m. (Sunday: 11 a.m. – 6 p.m.).
LOCATION On north bank of the river Thames at Hampton, south-west of London.

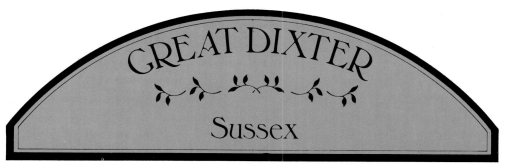

GREAT DIXTER

Sussex

The visitor, on his arrival at the garden gate of Great Dixter, may experience something of a surprise. No shaven lawn is there to greet him; no carefully tailored topiary; no billowing herbaceous border. All those features of an English garden are present, but they come later. The first thing the visitor to Great Dixter sees is an area of long grass – which at first glance looks like an unkempt field. But it is a field with a difference, and it is what Mr Christopher Lloyd calls his 'Meadow Garden – rough grass and wild flowers, to which suitable additions have been made. It is something we go in for in quite a big way. It disconcerts some visitors – the trim-minded ones, and delights others . . . My mother started it, and I have continued – *con amore*.'

In May, June and early July the 'Meadow Garden' at Great Dixter is very beautiful, starred as it is with tall daisies, cornflowers and poppies. But it is a highly sophisticated form of gardening, and without Mr Lloyd's expert eye, it could easily revert to hayfield and cease to be a garden at all. So it should be copied only with great care.'

Great Dixter is perhaps the most typically English garden one can think of. It was designed about sixty years ago by the eminent architect Sir Edwin Lutyens. It is not, therefore, a very old garden . . . yet, so happily is it married to the gabled house that it surrounds, that it seems far older than it is'. It is primarily a plantsman's garden, and there is no plant in the garden which is a dull or common plant. Furthermore, having been chosen with great knowledge by the owner Mr Christopher Lloyd, there are no plants which are not, probably, of the best variety available. 'So', it has been written, 'the garden might be legitimately described as approaching the ideal – an architect-designed garden planted by a connoisseur among gardeners. . . .' This is a rare combination.

The several gardens at Great Dixter lie all around the house. Each has its own character and its own atmosphere. They open, one from the other, like rooms in a house; one of the first on the visitors' tour is a sunk garden, luxuriously bordered with planting on three sides, and with a central lily pond, the fourth side being formed of a low out-building which in summer is completely embowered with vines, climbing plants and roses.

Out of this sunk garden, paved paths, with thickly planted borders on either side, lead under the walls of the house. In summer these borders are full of colour. Dahlias and Michaelmas daisies are to the fore, but these are inter-planted with fuchsias, plants once thought to be half-hardy – as indeed some are. Three of the most effective of these romantic, Victorian-looking flowers are the flesh-pink Lena, the red and mauve Display and the vigorous Madame

At Great Dixter there is a feeling of great luxuriance in all the planting.
Here herbaceous plants, interplanted with annuals, spill over a neatly paved path.
47

Cornelissen. With these are grown hebes – till recently known as veronicas – which come into their own in September, Autumn Glory and the pale mauve Midsummer Beauty being two of the most attractive.

From the flowers already mentioned, the impression might be given that the garden at Great Dixter is at its best in late summer and autumn. It would be a false impression. It is indeed a garden for all seasons, save, of course, winter, when, like all good gardens, it hibernates – though not for very long.

In February there are witch hazels and winter jasmines to lay their sweet scent on the still cold air, and the intrepid early iris. In March the first daffodils and earliest magnolias appear. In April come the species tulips, scillas and all the flowers of spring to take the eye with colour. In May the Meadow Garden comes into its own, and from then till the first frosts the garden is fairly bursting with colour and bloom. Recently a formal rose garden was made on the site of an old cattle yard. It is a new addition, and a most successful one.

Mr Christopher Lloyd is one of the most talented gardeners in England, and one of the best garden-writers we know. On his favourite subject he is always entertainingly articulate. When asked what were his favourite plants he replied:

It may sound snobbish, but I do like unusual plants. The storehouse of plant material that we can grow in these favoured islands is prodigiously rich, and yet is drawn upon so niggardly that I am continually goaded into championing things that should be seen more, like aciphyllas (the spear grasses of New Zealand), the South American sea holly (Eryngium pandanifolium), with its sea-green scimitar leaves, Zigadenus elegans, with sprays of starry green flowers, the bold-disced alpine thistle (Carlina acaulis), and Euphorbia wulfenii with its glaucous foliage and pale green flowering clusters in spring. If, as in all these cases, the plant has good, positive structure as well as subtle colouring so much the better.

Handsome foliage appeals to me very strongly; I would sell my soul for a shrub like the Cape Honey Flower (Melianthus major), and the fact of its being tender seems quite beside the point to me. Who would shirk the little bit of trouble needed on such a plant's behalf? And I am crazy about variegated foliage: a grass like Arundo donax variegata, or the sword leaves of a variegated yucca or of the green and yellow phormium; these plants make for big moments.

And yet I like the showy and the obvious as well, as a contrast, if not used indiscriminately and without imagination. I like dahlias and cannas, not in solid beds on their own, but taking their place among border plants and shrubs such as buddleias, hypericums, perovskias and caryopteris. In fact, I like mixing all categories of plants. It seems the natural thing to do. Their different habits act as foils one to another.

The garden at Great Dixter is different from most other British gardens in one most important respect. A great feature is made of annual plants. In these days of shortage of labour this is very rare: a few antirrhinums, perhaps, a modest show of petunias and tobacco flowers, but that is usually the sum. And yet how beautiful they are, and how much colour they bring to the garden at a moment when colour is sometimes on the wane. Mr Lloyd is adept at growing annuals and defends his taste for them.

The only difference between me and many other gardeners is that they cannot be bothered with the recurring business of sowing, pricking and planting out, whereas, to an extent, and in the interests of, say, the smell of mignonette and stocks, or of a good

RIGHT *A flower-filled courtyard in early summer.*

BELOW *Lilies and massed cornflowers by the front door.*

48

ABOVE *Michaelmas Daisies and grey-leaved Ballota pseudo-dictamnus make a striking contrast.*

ABOVE RIGHT *The well-planted mixed borders should brim over the edge of the path.*

LEFT *Fuchsias by the pool in the Autumn garden.*

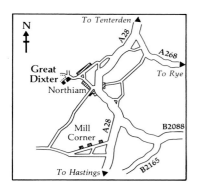

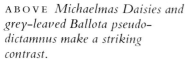

contrast in colour and form, I can. But I like biennials too: sweet williams and fox-gloves in particular, but, as these go over in July, it works well, I find, to sow some annuals such as cleomes in early May and have them coming on in readiness to take the biennials' place. Of course, another nice point about annuals and biennials is that you can take a rest from, and come back to them so easily. No major decisions have to be made as to what must be sacrificed or eliminated or worked up again by some long-winded propagation technique.

And so, thanks to the trouble that has been taken over the 'business of sowing, pricking and planting out', the garden at Great Dixter is bright, in season, with Salvia farinacea, a sage plant with mealy blue flowers and blue stems; with rudbeckias (cone flowers) such as the annual Autumn Glow, which has brilliant golden flowers; with the seldom-grown tithonia, from Mexico; and with spider flowers from the West Indies.

All this, as Mr Lloyd is ready to admit, takes a lot of time and hard work. His garden is an example of the achievement of a dedicated gardener. It has been planted with discrimination – and unique taste. It has been maintained by hard work. It has been cherished for years; in Mr Lloyd's words, *con amore*.

OPEN April 2nd – October 16th (approx): daily in the afternoon except Monday, open on Bank Holidays.
LOCATION In Northam village on A28 Hastings to Tenterden road, near junction of A28 and A268.

LEONARDSLEE
Sussex

The story of the garden at Leonardslee can be said to have begun when the twenty-seven-year-old Edmund Loder, athlete, big-game hunter, traveller, artist and winner of the School Prize at Eton, met and married Marion Hubbard, whose father lived at Leonardslee. This was in 1876. Some years after, Loder, who was soon to add botany to his many other interests, bought Leonardslee from his father in law. No sooner had he moved there than he set about planting the garden, while at almost the same time his brother, Gerald, began to plant the garden at Wakehurst, shown elsewhere in this book.

The situation at Leonardslee offered immense possibilities. It is still one of the most beautiful spots in the south of England, with the view from the house over a series of old Hammer and Furnace ponds, through vistas cut in St Leonards Forest, towards the Sussex Downs in the direction of the Roman camp at Chanctonbury Ring. Soon Edmund Loder was deep in the world of the rhododendron experts of that time and his garden could show a collection of rhododendrons second to none in the country. Year after year he produced hybrid plants of the highest quality. In one field, particularly, his zest and perseverance were spectacularly rewarded: by crossing R. griffithianum with the R. Fortunei, he produced a hybrid which was to sire some of the finest of all rhododendrons for gardens in the milder parts of England – the trumpet-flowered, deliciously fragrant R. Loderi. The flowering in 1907 of this remarkable new strain created something of a sensation. The varieties King George, Pink Diamond and Princess Marina are three of the finest. It might be said that it is these Loderi rhododendrons, many of them now of tree-like proportions, that make the chief fame of the garden at Leonardslee today.

When Sir Edmund, a man of tireless energy, died in 1920, a gardener at Leonardslee said, 'He used to near kill me some days in the garden, but now I don't know how I'll get on without him.' Sir Edmund was one of those great Victorian gardeners who, breaking away from the convention of his time – carpet-bedding and the like – recognized the possibilities of wild gardening in the way we understand it now. He had the eye of an artist and used it to create magnificent garden pictures with all the colours of the plant palette he had at his disposal. And yet, as he boldly planted the surroundings of his house with drifts of azaleas, rhododendrons and camellias, he took care not to destroy the wild character of his garden's woodland setting, and the best specimens of the existing trees were jealously guarded to give shelter and background to his new plants and more exotic plantations.

Rhododendrons, of course, are the plants which must always be most closely associated with the garden at Leonardslee, though there are many other

Azaleas make a bright vista of colour, leading the eye towards the Sussex woods beyond.

varieties there for both the horticulturist and the amateur to admire; it is a garden full of treasures which thrive in rather the same growing conditions as there are at the garden at Nymans, 'in another part of the forest'. Both domains lie in the thickly wooded part of Sussex which, in ancient times, was the thick forest in which St Leonard, it is said, killed the dragon. The lilies of the valley which carpet the ground every spring are said to have sprouted from where the monster's blood was shed.

The soil of the gardens at Leonardslee is a deep loam over sandstone and free from lime. The situation is well sheltered from the north, and the average rainfall is 28 inches a year. In short, it offers ideal growing conditions for camellias and magnolias, as well as rhododendrons. But besides these three great families of plants there are endless other interesting specimens at Leonardslee, such as trilliums, growing in drifts in the woods, odd three-petalled, three-leaved Wake Robins, which naturalize well in acid soil. There are Banksian roses, both the double and single varieties, growing on the house walls and filling the rooms inside with their scent. There are maples with bark like lacquer and maples (Acer Senkaki) with bark like coral; there are stewartias with flowers like camellias. But it is not intended, in these notes on Leonardslee, to name each of its shrubs or address each of its trees by name: the author would prefer the reader to treat these notes more as an introduction to the gardens and an encouragement to him to visit them and see them for himself.

ABOVE *Peltiphyllum peltatum, one of the saxifrage family, shows rosy flowers on tall snaky stems before its leaves appear.*

BELOW *A towering cedar and a bank of colour at Leonardslee.*

*Rhododendrons
at Leonardslee*

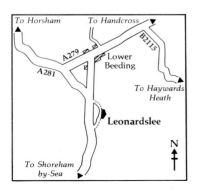

The author has visited the garden at Leonardslee several times. The first time was in April, when all the camellias were out, and he admired some plants of immense size. In the shelter of a wall C. reticulata Captain Rawes had grown over 16 feet high and was covered with deep rose flowers. The white Camellia nobilissima was already over, but Camellia donckelarii, so much more beautiful than its cumbersome name, was fully out, with its pink and white variegated flowers a joy to see. Some years ago Sir Giles and Lady Loder planted a trial ground of camellias where visitors to Leonardslee can now admire, and compare, several hundred clearly labelled varieties flowering side by side.

Camellias are, of course, members of the Theacae, the tea family. 'Thea' is how the sixteenth-century Dutch pronounced the Chinese word *T'e*, for which the classical Mandarin word was *Ch'a* – and whether one was in the army or not this has a familiar ring. Some plants of Thea sinensis grow and flower in the cool greenhouse at Leonardslee.

'Sir Edmund was an artist in the way he
clad the landscape . . . with colour.'

RIGHT *One of the sights of the garden
is a new camellia house. Though these
beautiful flowers thrive out of doors*

One interesting corner of the garden is devoted to the raising of dwarf conifers, those fascinating little trees which are so well suited to the smaller gardens of today. Two that especially take the visitor's eye are the flat-growing Pinus strobus prostrata, and Thuja occidentalis 'Hoveyi', with pale gold-green leaves. But the visitor who is interested in taller conifers should direct his or her steps to a particularly beautiful part of the garden called Mossy Ghyl. This is reached by stepping-stones over the stream. There the air is scented with azaleas, and a fine specimen of Picea breweriana excites the admiration. By some, Brewer's weeping spruce, with its lacy, pendant foliage, is considered to be the most beautiful conifer of all.

From the Ghyl a path leads downwards towards the old park and lower lake. This, we are told, was the setting used by Rudyard Kipling for the end of his story *Steam Tactics*. Kipling lived in Sussex and knew the garden at Leonardslee well.

'She . . . emerged into a fern glade fenced with woods so virgin, so untouched, that William Rufus might have ridden off as we entered.' 'Untouched' – for the planting of rhododendrons, camellias, and azaleas in the framework of old St Leonard's Forest has been so thoughtfully carried out as to appear quite natural, and Sir Edmund was an artist in the way he clad the landscape of Leonardslee with colour. Ninety years afterwards one can acclaim his taste and foresight. The gardens are some of the loveliest in England, and stand as a memorial to his creative skill.

The present owner, Sir Giles Loder, has said of Leonardslee, 'We . . . continually take a section of the garden in hand: cut down any old straggling plants . . . and replant with young up-to-date material. A garden must never stand still, and one has to look ahead for the future . . .' For gardeners everywhere it is good to know that Sir Edmund's taste and knowledge and devotion have been passed on to his grandson, who continues to love the gardens and look after them in spite of changing times and increasing difficulties.

OPEN End of April – beginning of June: Wednesday, Thursday, Saturday, Sunday, 10 a.m. – 6 p.m. Weekend mid – October for autumn colouring.
LOCATION On A281 in village of Lower Beeding, 4½ miles south-east of Horsham.

at Leonardslee, they appreciate the protection from wind and weather that glass affords.

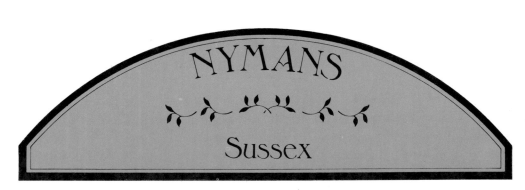

NYMANS

Sussex

The story of the garden at Nymans, today recognized as one of the most beautiful in the south of England, began nearly a century ago when the place was bought by Mr Ludwig Messel. At that time, the property lay in isolated countryside, far from the nearest railway station, and in a corner of Sussex which was difficult to get to in those far-off days before motor cars. Now a main road from London to Brighton, the M23, runs within a few hundred yards of the house, but once inside the garden, an extraordinary sense of peace falls on the visitor, the noise of the traffic fades to a soothing hum and the only apparent sound is the cooing of innumerable white pigeons.

Ludwig Mussel, who was an inspired gardener, had the almost ideal terrain to work on. There were the ancient trees of St Leonard's forest to shade and shelter his young plantations, a rich sandy loam in which his infant trees and shrubs could grow and, an essential to successful gardening, sharp drainage overall. The acid soil was perfect for magnolias, camellias and rhododendrons, which, though the garden has become rich in every other sort of rare and difficult tree and shrub, are the three plant families which remain the star attractions of the garden.

Nymans is famous too as the birth place of Eucryphia nymansensis, one of another beautiful family of flowering trees which revels in the very special growing conditions to be found in the garden. The Nymans eucryphia is the result of a cross, effected in 1915, between the evergreen Eucryphia cordifolia and the hardy, but deciduous Eucryphia glutinosa. Its garden value lies in its toleration, unlike most other eucryphias, of some lime in the soil, its shining evergreen leaves, its pure white, golden-anthered flowers, and its general hardiness inherited from its parent tree, Eucryphias glutinosa.

The gardens at Nymans are divided into many different sections, each with its own character and its own period of maximum attraction. To aid the visitor, attractive little folders are available and offer valuable advice, season by season, of where, at Nymans, the most telling plant pictures are to be found. At almost all seasons, every part of the garden has much to offer, but the Nymans folders make it easier for the visitor without a whole day at his disposal to make the very best of the time he has to spend.

The Spring Walk, for instance. This starts at a heraldic sculpture of a lion and passes under an arch of holly which must surely be one of the most impressive in the country. A wide field lies beyond, planted with naturalized narcissi and daffodils which, coming 'before the swallow dares', lay a golden carpet at the feet of the tall mixed conifers which half-surround them. Specially worthy of note in this area are a fine Japanese cedar (Cedrus spiralis) and a

In summer the borders fairly blaze – set off by four trees in elaborate topiary.

golden juniper (Juniperus aurea Youngii) of gleaming beauty. If it is April or May, there are rhododendrons all about in flower, and masses of azaleas to scent the air with their pungent perfume. Following the instructions in the Spring Walk Folder, the visitor then traces his way to the Lime Walk, and up-hill to the junction with the North Drive. From here the whole of Balcombe Forest, carpeted early in the year with anemones and primroses, can be surveyed. Back into the main garden, and the visitor is confronted with a collection of camellias second to none in the country, many of which were hybridized and raised at Nymans, and bear names, such as Leonard and Maud, of members of the Messel family. (Leonard Messel in particular has become a prestigious name in the gardening world, both Camellia Leonard Messel and the magnolia of the same name having won world-wide acclaim.) Near the camellias grow clumps of that loveliest of all small magnolias – Magnolia stellata – with starry, sweet-scented flowers and a compact habit of growth which makes it such a suitable plant for the smaller gardens of today. So the walk goes on, past the Prospect, with its balustrade and classic obelisks, built as a point of vantage, with a wonderful view over the surrounding park and woodland.

BELOW *An Italinate gateway of weathered brick in the walled garden. To the left, camellias for which the garden at Nymans is celebrated.*

BELOW RIGHT *Topiary trees with elaborate finials, by a fountain at the junction of four paths.*

Next on his verdant, flowery progress, the spring visitor to Nymans reaches the Sunk Garden, with an ancient Byzantine vase for centre-piece, and a brilliant planting of tulips rising from a blue haze of forget-me-nots. The heather garden lies nearby, and the rock garden, always full of colour in spring. It is in this area that some of the oldest trees planted by Leonard Messel are to be found – Cedars of Lebanon, 'Chief Champions of trees and forrestes', as the Scottish traveller, William Lithgow called them, and deodars from the slopes of the Himalayas. From this part of the garden there is a fine view of the house itself, and we might break off our walk to mention, with regret, that the house at Nymans is largely a ruin. This is the result of a disastrous fire about thirty years ago. Sad though that is, there are compensations; and the author of this book wrote, some years ago, 'Few gardens in England can have such a romantic background as is offered by the ruined house walls of Nymans, walls grey and calcined, with their glassless mullions curtained, but on the outside, with camellias, and with creamy Banksian roses climbing up to what were once the eaves, and red roses cascading down. . . .' But that was in summer time, and our Spring Walk is not yet completed. The Dovecote looks its best in May, grown all around with camellias, and with its conical roof a-flutter with white pigeons. Further on lies the walled garden, its herbaceous borders not yet in flower, but full of promise in spring, with their varying clumps of different greens. The walk makes its way under an Italian arch, wreathed in sweet-smelling Clematis armandii, and brings us back to the North Drive. Here are some of the great-leaved Chinese rhododendrons for which the garden at Nymans is famous – the yellow flowered Rhododendron macabeanum amongst them.

Such is the Spring Walk at Nymans. There are Summer and Autumn Walks as well. All three offer endless treats, and the attractive folders describing them make them easy to follow and to enjoy.

The garden at Nymans is a very great garden indeed. It is full of rare plants, delicate and seldom-grown shrubs, unusual trees. But though it is of absorbing interest to the connoisseur, it is far from being merely a plantsman's garden. Room in it has been found for all of the best loved, simple flowers of England. 'Rarities which can only be addressed in Latin, but Lady's Smocks too', fox-gloves, bergamot and bluebells, as well as rhododendrons from the distant uplands of Burma.

OPEN April – October: Tuesday, Wednesday, Thursday, Saturday 2 p.m. – 7 p.m. (or sunset). Sundays and Bank Holiday Mondays: 11 a.m. – 7 p.m. (or sunset). Last admission 1 hour before closing.
LOCATION South-east edge of Handcross on B2114 (off London to Brighton A[M]23 road). Signposted.

LEFT *Informally laid paving, a stone vase and pots of flowers in the courtyard of Nymans.*

ABOVE *The very picture of spring.*
Daffodils and hanging sprays
of cherry blossom.

*Wakehurst Place was built in the last decade
of Queen Elizabeth I's reign.*

WAKEHURST PLACE
Sussex

Wakehurst Place, near Ardingly, was built by Sir William Culpeper in the last decade of the reign of Queen Elizabeth I. Its picturesque façade with its gabled wings and many windows, is typical of late Elizabethan architecture, when the fortified manor house or castle was giving way, owing to securer times, to more sophisticated building. Sir William chose the site for his new house on rising ground, and the view that his mullioned windows command is as fair a prospect as any in Sussex.

Wakehurst has been owned by many families, and it is outside the scope of this book to trace the story of the house in detail. Its garden history may be said to begin when the occupants were the Boord family, who restored the house and created much of the garden that we see today. In the '90s of the last century the Lady Boord of the moment was a keen gardener, and it was she who laid out the rock garden at Wakehurst which is still such a feature. Many of the shrubs and small trees still growing in this part of the garden she planted herself – and that at a time when few English women took more than a remote interest in gardening and, far from handling a spade themselves, confined their activities to giving complicated instructions to their gardeners.

From the Boords, Wakehurst passed to the Loder family. Loder is a name famous in the gardening world, and it was given to some of the most beautiful of scented rhododendrons, the Loderi strain, which are described in the chapter on Leonardslee.

Sir Gerald Loder's speciality, besides rhododendrons, was plants which originated in the Antipodes and in South America, Chile in particular. For this sort of plant, the climate and terrain of Wakehurst provided almost perfect growing conditions, with light woodland, abundant water from lake and streams, and tall forest trees for windbreaks. In due course, Sir Gerald was made Lord Wakehurst, and during his lifetime the garden became one of the sights of Sussex. On his death, the estate passed to Sir Henry Price, and in 1963 the gardens, by way of the National Trust, came under the direction of the Royal Botanic Gardens at Kew, who, for some years, had been looking for a 'satellite' garden. Wakehurst Place, with its clean air, moisture, and above all, acid soil, offered vastly better and more varied growing conditions than those at Kew, where, for instance, rhododendrons do not thrive.

Some of the rare plants which the plant connoisseur should look for are the late-flowering Rhododendron eriogynum, which was discovered in Yunnan by George Forrest in 1914; the Chilean Berberidopsis corallina, a scarlet-flowered climber which is at its best in late summer; a Chinese conifer which is seldom seen in Britain, Keteleeria davidiana, which actually produces its rare cylindrical cones at Wakehurst; and the sub-tropical Japanese evergreen Litsea glauca, with clusters of whitish flowers. One of the most interesting antipodean plants to be seen is the cone-bearing Phyllocladus trichomanoides, once used by the Maoris of New Zealand to produce a bright red dye.

Wakehurst is a garden for almost all seasons. High moments are early spring, when the azaleas are in flower and the air is laden with their scent. In early summer the rock-garden, legacy of Lady Boord's work eighty years ago, is bright with flower, and saxifrages, sempervivums and helianthemums (good plants for the smallest garden, as well as for the largest) are in their first burst of colour.

It has been written, 'At a time in our history when the future of any garden the size of Wakehurst must be in doubt, it is reassuring to find such a great garden, the future of which, in the doughty care of Kew, is certainly assured.'

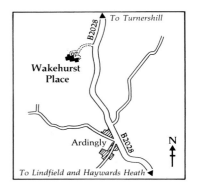

OPEN Daily: 10 a.m. – 4 p.m. in winter except Christmas and New Year's Day, 10 a.m. – 7 p.m. in summer.
LOCATION 1 mile north of Ardingly village on B2028 Turners Hill road.

RIGHT *Papaver orientale. The Oriental Poppy shows as brilliant a red as any flower in horticulture. Beyond, the budding spires of delphiniums.*

BELOW LEFT *The soil and terrain of the garden at Wakehurst is ideal for many rare plants which do not thrive at Kew. To the left, behind the bridge, a flower-covered bush of Viburnum tomentosum.*

BELOW *The many colours of the garden in autumn are duplicated in the lake.*

2

WALES AND THE WEST

CRANBORNE MANOR
Dorset

One of the first gardeners in England to achieve international fame was John Tradescant (d. 1638). Two well known plants are named after him: Tradescantia virginiana, the spider flower, an old-fashioned herbaceous plant; and Tradescantia fluminensis, 'wandering Jew', a trailing indoor plant with white and green striped leaves, often to be found on office-workers window sills. It is on record that John Tradescant made the original plan for the garden at Cranborne soon after the present Manor was built by the Cecil family in the seventeenth century.

The garden at Cranborne Manor retains much of John Tradescant's original layout, two still-existing features of which are the Bowling-alley and the Mound, a fashionable feature of Jacobean Gardens; the latter is now planted as a garden of old roses, with such telling names as Pale Pink Moss, Variegata di Bologna, Fantin Latour and Gypsy Boy.

Cranborne Manor garden is essentially English. Roses flower everywhere over a fragrant undergrowth of herbs such as lavender, rosemary and rue. One particular corner is a favourite of Lady Salisbury, a passionate and well informed gardener, who herself works for long hours among her flowers. This favoured part she calls '. . . the Sweet Garden; for it is largely a herb garden and full of flowers and savours, and clothed even in winter because of the numbers of evergreen and evergrey herbs: it is delicious to work in, as the various scents cling to one throughout the day.'

Another favourite part of the garden is the North Court, which has newly been planted with white flowers, with some touches of cream and apricot.

The Manor itself is the dominating feature of the garden at Cranborne, and from every angle its pearly grey walls, hung with pink and yellow roses, make a perfect backdrop. The north and south façades of the house are embellished with two classical porches, and there is good reason to suppose them the work of the great architect Inigo Jones, who is known to have worked at nearby Wilton. The north porch is the most elaborate and giving, as it does, on to the flower-filled terrace, seems as integral a part of the garden as a gazebo or summer house might be. The porch is strongly Italianate in feeling, and above each of its four pillars is a gaping mask, 'perhaps more grotesque than beautiful, which adds an endearing light-hearted touch to architectural nicety'.

Recently another and quite modern attraction has been added to those already enhancing Cranborne. This is an extremely efficiently run Garden Centre, where many of the very special plants the visitor admires in the borders can be bought. Silver-leaved plants, such as artemisia, santolina and senecio, so popular with gardeners today, are a speciality.

Bright twin borders of pinks, pansies and annual flowers.

One last remark about Cranborne might add to the interest of the garden, especially to visitors who are not exclusively garden-conscious. The terrace (one of the four, incidentally, to survive from the very early seventeenth century) was the scene, in the well known film, of Tom Jones' departure from home to make his fortune.

OPEN First weekend each month April – October (Saturdays all day, Sunday 2 p.m. – 6 p.m.). Also open on Bank Holiday Mondays, 10 a.m. – 6 p.m.
LOCATION 10 miles north of Wimborne on Salisbury road.

A picture which seems to catch the varied scents of summer. In the foreground, honeysuckle.

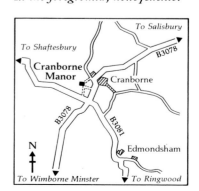

ABOVE *Old roses and foxgloves in midsummer.*

TOP *The twin lodges on either side of the court-yard entrance date from James I's day.*

RIGHT *Against the old church tower of Cranborne, blue campanulas show their bright bell-flowers.*

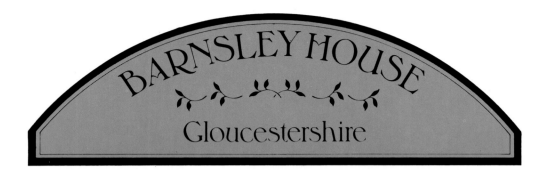
Barnsley House is just in the village of Barnsley, between Cirencester and Bibury. It stands back on a slight eminence, on the right as one comes from Cirencester. There are late eighteenth-century stone gate-posts under over-hanging yews, at the drive entrance. A sweep of lawn rises diagonally across the front of the house to an eighteenth-century Gothick summer-house; but the front itself is terraced and is built on the site of a Roman road. This is almost the last small valley on the eastern edge of the Cotswolds, a valley without a river but where all the houses are built of honey-coloured stone. On the garden side of the house the land is flat as far as the eye can see, as it stretches into the Oxford plain.

Mr and Mrs David Verey moved to Barnsley in 1951, when the house was given to them by Mr Verey's parents who had bought it in 1939. Before that it had been the rectory. There was a wonderful surrounding stone wall, built in 1771 by the Rev. Charles Coxwell, and the charming north-facing Gothick summer-house he had made for his wife, known as Mrs Coxwell's 'alcove'; and also a ha-ha and perimeter trees planted about 1840 by another contributing rector. There were broad herbaceous borders, rather far from the house, backed by yew hedges newly planted in 1939. The hedges grew up during the war and now define the area of a small arboretum and the swimming pool and aviaries. The ha-ha had to be blocked out by a beech hedge, as a visual pro-tection against proposed but now unlikely road developments. Happily this hedge gives the garden a satisfactory feeling of enclosure, as well as being a great deterrent to the prevailing west wind.

Gradually as Mrs Verey's interest in gardening increased, the vegetables were banished to a situation outside the wall and a new vista or *allée*, the length of the wall, was created parallel to the house but invisible from it. In 1962 a late eighteenth-century Tuscan temple was added to the garden as an 'eye-catcher' at one end of the new *allée*. For the other end, a fountain by Simon Verity was specially commissioned. On one side of the *allée* are broad mixed borders, on the other a lime walk which develops into a laburnum tunnel. In front of the temple there is a goldfish pond and a paved garden enclosed by an early nineteenth-century wrought-iron screen. The axis of the *allée* is crossed by a path which is bordered with Irish yews and leads directly from the garden door in the south-east front of the house, dated 1697, to a wrought-iron gate in the wall, which takes one to the kitchen garden and tennis court. This path is the central feature of a parterre with lawns and four shaped borders.

Beyond the southern corner of the house there is a newly planted small knot garden in front of an early nineteenth-century Gothick veranda. This and the

RIGHT *A stone path grown thickly with different coloured Rock Roses (helianthemum) runs between Irish Yews towards the grey stone face of Barnsley House.*

BELOW *A closely-set border with the bright yellow leaves of oreganum (Marjoram) in front of the rosy purple flowers of Erysimum linifolium, a perennial wall-flower.*

castellations on the front porch and bay window were all part of an attempt to make the house look more Tudor in 1830, a fashionable trend of the time.

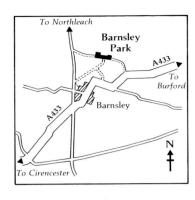

The Vereys have tried to give each part of the garden its own character so that there is a change of mood as you go round. Even if it is too uninviting to walk in the garden on winter days, one does use the drive, so it is there that they have concentrated on the winter and early spring flowers. There is a mass of aconites; clumps of stinking hellebore (Helleborus foetidus), whose apple-green flowers give weeks of pleasure; snowdrops; scillas; pale blue pushkinias; dark blue grape hyacinths; and yellow and white large-flowered crocus. Small clumps of autumn- and spring-flowering cyclamen grow there too, and are increasing. All these make carpets under the one-hundred-year-old trees – planes, limes and chestnuts – which flank one side of the drive. But to keep the entrance inviting all the year, the terraces have been given a formal look with a row of dark upright Chamaecyparis Elwoodii alternating with grey mounds of santolina. Clipped box softens the contours of the house itself.

This mixture of formal with informal has been repeated through the whole garden. In the straight path between the Irish yews is a mass of pink rock roses in May and June. Tucked between the laburnum tunnel and the wall, a shady walk has a patterned red brick path and two narrow box-edged borders full of bulbs and polyanthus, followed by ferns, foxgloves and mulleins. The laburnums, in full flower in the first two weeks of June, are underplanted with hostas, alliums and hellebores, and make one of the most attractive garden pictures imaginable.

In mixed borders plants are used which give a long display such as hebes, potentillas and penstemons, 'greys' and euphorbias, while for bold effects there

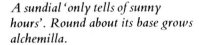

A sundial 'only tells of sunny hours'. Round about its base grows alchemilla.

A newly-planted Knot Garden, of lavender, santolina, box and rosemary. When more established the rosemary hedge will be clipped formally.

are acanthus, seakale (Crambe cordifolia), eremurus, yuccas and New Zealand flax (Phormium tenax). Everywhere the aim is to keep the ground well covered to minimize weeding, but even more important, to create a feeling of completion.

The deciduous shrubs are underplanted with bulbs and spring-flowering pulmonarias, symphytum and lots of forget-me-nots. Variegated honeysuckle and ivies are used as ground-covering clumps at the front of the borders. A June feature are the groups of Jacob's ladder (Polemonium caeruleum) with 3-foot spikes of rich blue flowers; these were grown from seed brought back from Palestine.

77

Visitors to Barnsley often say how peaceful the pond and temple garden are, the *allées* are to walk in, but this garden is to sit quietly in, beneath the shade of a quince, a silver birch, a Eucalyptus gunnii and a mop-headed standard Buddleia alternifolia, always a mass of scented pale mauve flowers in June. Other good scents are provided by tree paeonies, rosemary growing up the wall (in the Tudor fashion), Buddleia fallowiana and tubs of lilies, lemon verbenas and scented-leaf geraniums.

There are pots and tubs at the garden doors and on the veranda – always generously planted. For spring they have several layers of bulbs; crocuses on top, hyacinths a bit lower, then early narcissus like Peeping Tom and February Gold, and below them usually a few special tulips. The summer tubs on the terrace have old standard lemon verbenas as their central features surrounded by dark pink ivy-leafed geraniums, cherry pie and grey and gold-leafed Helichrysum petiolatum. The secret would seem to be to fill them full; the plants then support and protect each other, and look luxuriant.

The Italian pots on the veranda are filled with the lavender ivy-leafed geranium mixed with 'greys' and more scented geraniums. Echeverias, a Victorian bedding favourite, are allowed to multiply in their pots, spilling down the sides and forming metallic grey rosettes nearly a foot across. From the veranda you can look down on the knot garden which was planted in May 1975 and is now showing a well defined pattern. The designs come, one from a French book of 1583, and the other from a 1664 English book. The interlacing threads are made with dark green and variegated box and lavender. They are enclosed by a rosemary hedge, and there are clipped holly, lavender cotton and phillyrea, all Elizabethan plants.

Much time and thought is spent on the walls. The longest, facing north-west, gets the afternoon sun, and there is always space for another clematis, favourites such as the spring alpina and macropetala and the later texensis, Gravetye Beauty. There are several honeysuckles and evergreen shrubs to keep the Cotswold stone well clothed in winter. Piptanthus, Itea ilicifolia, Jasminum revolutum and the variegated form of Pittosporum tenuifolium are not climbers but do appreciate the extra winter protection.

A small arboretum rewards a visit. The first planting of trees in 1962 were chosen for spring blossom and autumn colour and fruits, and some like the ginkgo, wellingtonia and cedar are for future generations. Sorbus do so well on the Cotswold limestone and provide berries ranging from white and yellow to pink, red and mahogany brown.

Plants are readily propagated in the mist propagator at Barnsley, and as at Bampton Manor there is a good selection of container grown shrubs, herbs and grey plants for sale. 'And', says Mrs Verey, 'for gardeners who are just starting it is a great help to see things growing in the garden before they buy them. Another pleasure is meeting many of the visitors who come here. Our conversations will often stimulate interesting suggestions and exchange of plants and seeds. I have made many good friends that way.'

OPEN Every Wednesday: 12 a.m. – 6 p.m. First Sunday in May, June, July: 2 p.m. – 7 p.m.
LOCATION 4 miles north-east of Cirencester on A433 Burford road.

A tunnel of laburnum shades a closely-paved path.
On either side the purple heads of Allium aflatunense.

HIDCOTE MANOR
Gloucestershire

Hidcote Manor lies in the very heart of England in that quiet green countryside on the borders of Gloucestershire and Worcestershire. It was bought in 1907 by an American, Colonel Lawrence Johnston, who at once set about planning and planting a garden there which was to found a new school of gardening in England.

The site was not promising. True, it had lovely views over Alfred Housman's 'coloured counties', but it offered few of those ready-made features which can be so helpful to the gardener who is planning his garden from scratch, such as old stone walls – oddly enough, for Hidcote is near the Cotswolds. The site was bare and exposed to all the winds of heaven. There were some good beech trees, one fine cedar, and little else. Lawrence Johnston was a courageous man and full of imagination when he studied, like Lancelot Brown, the 'capabilities' of the terrain and remained undaunted.

How was it then that Johnston was so successful, and made a garden which within a few years was to be something of a sensation in gardening circles? First, he planted windbreaks, for the site was very exposed; and the hedges he planted were different from any that English garden-makers had ever planted before. There were yew hedges, it is true, but there were less conventional hedges as well. There was a hedge of copper beech, glowing dark red in the sunshine. There was one of silver euonymus (spindle) and a hedge of mingled yew and box, with the matt and shining greens in contrast. The most spectacular of Colonel Johnston's hedges at Hidcote was a 'tapestry' hedge, his own invention, in which yew, holly and beech are combined, to show in summer 'a marbled surface of several greens, and in winter one of greens splashed with foxy brown'. Was his inspiration for his tapestry hedge the motley appearance of almost any English hedgerow? It probably was, because Lawrence Johnston had the gift of grouping quite ordinary plants together and creating a very special picture.

The second novelty in the garden at Hidcote was the way the hedges were used: not, as was usual at that time, to line an avenue or shut off some unpleasing view, but to create outdoor 'rooms', walled with closely-clipped leaves but open to the sky. This was a new concept in gardening – especially in 1907, the hey-day of long vistas, of the wide croquet lawn and, first and foremost, of the herbaceous border.

The garden at Hidcote is planned rather like a house with a central hall or passage-way and rooms, each with its own character, opening to left and right.

The visitor to the garden enters through a courtyard under the walls of the house. These walls, of the beautiful dove-coloured stone of the Cotswolds, are

Shrubs are mixed with flowers
in a brimming border.

hung with climbers: in season, the purple and gold flowers of the Chilean potato tree (Solanum crispum), exotic cousin of our own potato, light up the scene, while a dark corner is illuminated at a lower level by the yellow butter-cup flowers of the Hypericum patulum which was first raised at Hidcote, and which today bears its name. Nearby a lofty bush of Hydrangea heteromalla shows its lacy flowers. Through another gate, and the visitor is in the main part of the garden itself, with the high cedar towering before him – the cedar which was the only ready-made feature that Lawrence Johnston originally found.

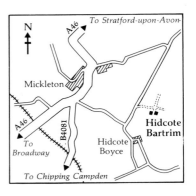

To describe each of the smaller gardens-within-a-garden at Hidcote in detail would demand a slim volume rather than a few pages. But these are some which the visitor should specially look for. The pool garden first. This is surrounded by hedges of close-cropped yew – streaked with the scarlet of the climbing flame flower (Tropaeolum speciosum). Almost its whole area is taken up by a lily pond, of which the surrounding walls are raised, bringing the level of the water with its floating lilies, and flashing fish, to an almost companionable level.

Another garden at Hidcote is planted in shades of silver and gold, with the lily flowers of Yucca filamentosa rising above the frothy green lace of Lady's Mantle (Alchemilla mollis) and tall evening primrose (oenothera) nodding shoulder high at the path's edge. As the visitor brushes past them he feels among friends. Round the corner is yet another garden with the tall spires of the peach-leaved bellflower (Campanula persicifolia) echoing the shape of the pyramid-shaped yews amongst which they are planted.

In the rose garden there is a collection of old shrub roses, of which the French names are always so charming – Reine des Violettes, Coupe D'Hebe and Boule de Neige. Of the roses at Hidcote, that great gardener and friend of the author of this book, Victoria Sackville-West (creator, with her husband, of the beauti-ful garden at Sissinghurst), has written in her own vibrant style: 'It would take pages to enumerate them all, so let me merely revive the memory of that June day, and the loaded air, and the bushes weeping to the ground with the weight of their own bloom, a rumpus of colour, a drunkenness of scents.'

Another part of the garden at Hidcote is completely different. No flowers. No shrubs. No roses to lay their sweetness on the air. But it is an area which only a gardener with an artist's eye could have conjured – a large, perfectly proportioned stretch of turf, which Colonel Johnston called his Theatre Lawn. At the far end, on a rising grassy platform, stand, in solemn consultation, some spreading beech trees. If we have likened the enclosed gardens of Hidcote to rooms in a house – this lawn must surely be the ball-room, with its dance floor of smooth turf, and its orchestra platform, or stage, at one end. It is simplicity – the reliance on scale and on emptiness for its effect – that the Theatre Lawn at Hidcote displays to the full, the planning genius of that great gardener, Lawrence Johnston, who came to love England, and made his home there.

OPEN Easter Saturday or April 1st (whichever is earlier) to end of October: 11 a.m. – 8 p.m. Last admission 7 p.m., or an hour before dusk, if earlier. Closed Tuesday and Friday.
LOCATION Turning to Hidcote Bartrim off Mickleton – Shipston-on-Stour road.

RIGHT *Throughout the garden there is a strong architectural feeling, here supplied by clipped hornbeams (Carpinus betulus) contrasting with lower hedges of of yew and box.*

BELOW *A view which shows clearly the special charm of the series of gardens which make up the one beautiful garden at Hidcote Manor. In the distance, the pool garden.*

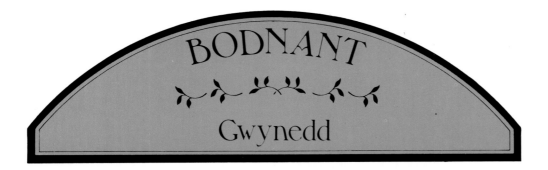

BODNANT
Gwynedd

Bodnant, home for generations of the Aberconway family, has a famous garden in an absolutely ideal setting. Its site is a leafy valley, falling gently to the south, with Britain's grandest mountain, Snowdon, beyond. The Lords Aberconway have been great gardeners for nearly a century, and they were quick to realize that their Welsh domain, well watered, splendidly timbered and sheltered from the north, could soon become the home of a thousand rare and tender plants.

From the house, the garden falls in five great terraces, each with its own character and planting, towards the Conway valley. *Genii loci* of the first terrace are a pair of sphinxes, whose heads, turned sharply to one side in a most unusual way, meet the visitor with a stare, perhaps of surprise that their solitude should be disturbed. But all else is welcoming indeed, and two splendid arbutus, with glistening, dark green leaves and reddish bark, fairly glow in the clear Welsh sunlight. Steps, overhung in early summer with the tassels of a white Wistaria venusta, lead downward to a second terrace, used for a croquet lawn. In the surrounding borders, sheltered by the terrace walls, grow fine specimens of Eucryphia nymansensis, the miniature lilac Syringa microphylla and the low-growing, sweet-smelling Daphne tangutica.

On the third terrace there is a lily pond – vast in extent and in part shaded by two cedars, one the frosty blue Cedrus Atlantica glauca and the other a cedar of Lebanon – Cedrus Libani. Again, in the shelter of the terrace walls, the plant connoisseur recognizes such rarities as the pink Buddleia Colvilei and the seldom met with Photinia glomerata.

Next comes the fourth terrace, reached by shallow, well designed steps, which seem to fit the foot instead of wilfully deceiving it as do so many badly designed garden steps. Here are more rare shrubs, or if not rare, the very best garden varieties of popular plants – the Glasnevin variety of the Potato Vine (Solanum crispum), for instance. Nearby, is the rose garden 'neatly bedded and pathed, and decorated with sturdy pergolas of trellis-work, capped with wooden urns. The design for these was taken, unexpectedly enough, from the garden of the Ritz Hotel in London.'

The fifth and lowest terrace provides the visitor with the most spectacular view in the garden at Bodnant: the Pin Mill, an enchanting little eighteenth-century building, rescued by the Lord and Lady Aberconway of the day from imminent demolition in distant Gloucestershire. Before it, and to mirror its architectural perfection, lies a glassy canal, studded but not overgrown with lilies, which are kept well to one end so as not to mar reflections.

These, then, are the five terraces of Bodnant, one of the really great gardens

RIGHT *Below the gabled house there is a Baroque-looking fountain, grown round with wistaria.*

BELOW *A feature of the garden at Bodnant is the Pin-Mill – an elegant little eighteenth century building rescued, when a near ruin, from a village in Gloucestershire where it had last been used as a pin-factory. At Bodnant it is reflected in a canal with water lilies.*

ABOVE *A seat, painted a subtle shade of bluish-black, in the shelter of perfectly clipped yew hedges.*

LEFT *A stream with azaleas in the tree-shaded dell.*

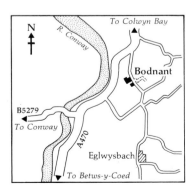

of Britain. Lists of Latin plant names can be tedious, but the garden abounds in rarities. Magnolias kobus, salicifolia robusta, and the later-flowering sieboldii, offer in turn their scented chalices of flower. By the stream, primulas show their many-coloured spires of flower, and the Himalayan blue poppy rivals the colour of the sky. But Bodnant is a garden for all visitors: there is much to delight and fascinate the plantsman; there are garden-pictures on every hand to seduce the artist.

One last feature of the garden must not be omitted. On the lowest terrace, and at the far end of the canal to the Pin Mill is a 'green theatre' with raised stage of turf, and wings and back-drop of closely clipped yew. If ever there was the perfect setting for *A Midsummer Night's Dream* it must surely be here.

OPEN April – October: daily, except Friday and some Sundays. 1.30 p.m. – 5 p.m. (Visitors should check before going.)
LOCATION 8 miles south of Llandudno and Colwyn Bay off A470 (A496). Entrance $\frac{1}{2}$ mile along Eglwysbach road.

A statue set in a neatly clipped hedge of box,
below one of the balustraded terraces.

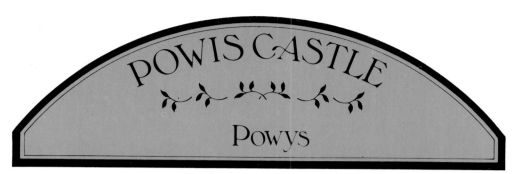

POWIS CASTLE
Powys

The garden at Powis Castle is, in the opinion of the writer of this book, one of the two or three really great gardens of Britain. It seems to have every quality which a great garden requires – history, a perfect site, maturity, fine trees, well chosen plants, good architecture, good statuary, water and last, but by no means least, owners who have loved and looked after it for centuries. In having all these attributes, the garden at Powis must be almost unique.

The Castle is set on a high bluff chosen by old Welsh princes, in almost pre-historic times, on account of its impregnable position.

The guide book to the Castle itself admirably sets out the history of the place – the owners of Powis have often changed in the seven or more hundred years of its existence; and the different families who have lived there, and their stories, lie outside the scope of a book about gardens. Suffice it to say that the first gardening family to inhabit the Castle was almost certainly the Dutch Earl of Rochford and his son Lord Enfield, who occupied the castle for some thirty years after William III became King, while the Powis family themselves, ardent Jacobites, were in exile.

During their short tenure, the Rochfords certainly built the terraces, which are the most striking feature of the garden at Powis today; and they probably planted the yews, visible as well established but still small trees in an old print of the Castle dated 1742. They are now enormous, and like the terraces, imposing features of the garden.

In due course the Powis family were allowed to return to their ancient home, and their heiress, Lady Henrietta Herbert, married the son of the celebrated Lord Clive. It is their descendants who still live at Powis, and it was Henrietta's grandson, the third Earl of Powis, who planted the rare trees and shrubs collected from all over the world which are the glory of the garden today and make it so fascinating botanically.

The garden faces south-east, and though it is 450 feet above sea level benefits to some extent by the Gulf Stream which just touches the north coast of Wales – plants thrive there as they would not further inland, and this is due not only to the remote blessing of the Gulf Stream but also to the perfect drainage of the site of moisture and, almost more important, of frost. It is a recognized fact that cold, frosty air, weighing more than warm air, flows down a hill like water, collecting in hollows and valleys, which can then become harmful 'frost pockets'. This is a well proven theory, and the garden at Powis is an excellent example of it. It is some miles from the sea, and yet delicate shrubs and trees will flourish there which would not survive in similar latitudes inland.

The visitor to Powis is at once impressed by the taste and original thought shown in the planting of the garden, and of the different terraces. Entering by a gate in the lower garden, his or her eye is at once arrested by a pair of Victorian *jardinieres* in basket form, set high on pillars, and planted, not, as so often, with tired and thirsty-looking geraniums, but with white fuchsias and soaring dracaenas. These well planted pots seem to be a recurring theme in the garden, and some, indeed, do contain geraniums – but they are geraniums with a difference: some with crinkled, scented leaves; some with leaves that are marbled; and all with a well fed, well watered appearance which speaks of constant care on the part of the garden staff.

The flowerbeds at Powis seem to be planted with a special opulence One is thickly set with heliotrope, silver cineraria and lilies. Another bed is 'entirely given over to musk roses, with all their lovely girl-names, Penelope, Felicia and Cornelia, clearly labelled, a rare touch in gardens and a very useful one in gardens open to the public'. It is only a pity that visitors should so often reward the garden-owners' thought by removing the labels as souvenirs.

At Powis, fuchsias seem to be favourite plants; not only tender varieties in pots, but also the hardy F. Riccartonii and the beautiful F. megallanica versicolor. There is a whole bed of this lovely fuchsia under the walls of the Castle, its smoky-pink foliage blending beautifully with the soft pink of the stonework.

ABOVE *Fuchsias in a Victorian basket-work pot of terra-cotta, with a view of the Welsh hills beyond.*

RIGHT *A garden stair in the grandest manner. On the bottom pillars are basket-work pots of different geraniums, and soaring dracaenas.*

On the Aviary Terrace there are fine plants of Rosa rubrifolia, with its ruby-coloured leaves, and of the seldom-planted Clerodendron fargesii from China, which gives such a good display in autumn with its shining porcelain blue berries. On the Aviary Terrace, too, and one wonders if that is how it got its name, is a lead figure of a peacock, said to have been brought back to England from India by the great Lord Clive.

The garden at Powis is full of rare plants, and a too-long list of botanical names can become daunting. A few, however, cannot, in any survey of the garden, be overlooked: Pittosporum tenuifolium and Hoheria lyallii from New Zealand; Drimys winteri, the magnolia-like Winter's Bark from South America; the blue passion flower (Passiflora coerulea); the orange trumpet climber (Campsis radicans); and the Chilean Abutilon vitifolium, of which the deep violet blue variety A. v. suntense is so spectacularly the best.

Below the terraces, there is a gently sloping bank 'planted with more flowering trees and shrubs which take the eye with blossom, and spread their differing sweetness on the air'. Trees such as the exquisite Magnolia Wilsonii, from Szechuan in China, two splendid (and rarely seen) dogwoods (Cornus chinensis) with white flowers flushed with red as they mature, Feijoa sellowiana and the white Banksian rose. In the autumn, Cercidiphyllum japonicum bursts into dying fire, so brightly coloured are its leaves.

Round the pool at Powis grow gunnera, like giant rhubarbs, the imposing but evil smelling arum (Lysichitum americanum), well named skunk cabbage, and the royal fern, such as we see at Scotney, Osmunda regalis. On the sky-line, stands the tallest tree in Britain, a Douglas fir, which, when last measured, was 181 feet high.

One more feature of the garden must be noticed before, with regret, we make our way – the lead figures on the balustrade of the second terrace. These are by the celebrated Jan Van Nost, and represent shepherds and shepherdesses. They were brought to the garden by the Dutch Lord Rochford two hundred and sixty years ago, and have been there ever since.

The history of the castle itself, the grandeur of its terraces and the consummate taste in the planting of the garden make a visit to Powis a memorable event. Fortunately, protected by the shield of the National Trust, there is reasonable hope that the garden may continue in beauty for years to come. It is one of the greatest of British gardens.

LEFT *The lead statues at Powis are by Jan van Nost, who lived from 1668 to 1729.*

BELOW LEFT *The terraces, with their lead statues, are a happy marriage of weathered brick and finely-cut stone.*

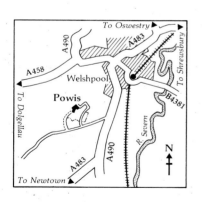

OPEN May 1st – September 30th: daily (except Monday and Tuesday): 2 p.m. – 6 p.m. Wednesday, Sunday in July and August: Gardens open 11.30 a.m. – 6 p.m. Bank Holidays: Easter Saturday, Sunday, Monday: 2 p.m. – 6 p.m. Spring and Late Summer Bank Holiday Monday: 11.30 a.m. – 6 p.m.
LOCATION South of Welshpool on A483. Turn right after 1 mile.

TRESCO ABBEY
Isles of Scilly

Over 110 years ago, the Lord Proprietor of the Isles of Scilly, Mr Augustus Smith, wrote to a lady friend in England, describing some of the plants in his garden and how they were doing. The puya showed signs of flowers, but as yet the aloe did not. Chamaerops excelsa (a sort of palm tree) and the dwarf palm (C. humilis) were in full bud, and he had forests of dracaenas and beschornerias in full blossom.

Anyone with a vague knowledge of plants will recognize at once that the plants Mr Smith mentioned are all of the greatest rarity and delicacy. At that date, Puya alpestris probably flowered in the open nowhere else in England; chamaerops was less rare, but still uncommon; and dracaenas, and especially beschornerias, being natives of the Canary Islands and of the hot plains of Mexico respectively, were extremely uncommon plants to find in any garden. The garden at Tresco was full of such rarities over a century ago, and still is. It is certainly the only garden in Britain in which so many sub-tropical plants can be grown in the open.

The island of Tresco is the second largest of the Scilly group, and lies forty miles out into the Atlantic, off the Cornish mainland. When Augustus Smith came there, in the thirties of the last century, the island was wild and almost uninhabited, swept by wind, and bare of trees except for a few poor specimens which just survived in the garden of the vicarage. But the island cast a potent spell, and a Bishop of Truro, following a fleeting visit, described it as having '. . . a wonderful freshness in the air . . . the colours of the white sand, the blue and sapphire sea, the golden sea weed, the Sea Pinks, the gorse and heather, have the freshness of a jewel'.

Augustus Smith, a natural gardener, who understood perfectly the needs of plants, realized at once the possibilities of making a garden at Tresco, bleak and windswept as it might at first appear. He recognized that the climate was blessed, as the climate in no other part of Britain was, by the warm breath of the Gulf Stream, and that the island was seldom blighted by frost. All that was needed were walls and windbreaks, and these he started at once to build and plant. Within a few years he had his first successes, and soon rare plants from all over the world were spreading their leaves and showing their flowers as they might have done in gardens a thousand miles to the south.

The garden at Tresco is divided into three lengthwise by the Top Terrace, the shorter Middle Terrace, and lowest of all, the Long Walk, which is the main axis of the garden. The Lighthouse Walk acts as cross-axis, and this runs to the Neptune Steps, presided over by a stone head of the sea god himself. The garden is celebrated the world over for the rare plants which grow in it. More

Neptune's steps, curtained and cushioned with geraniums and sun-loving mesembryanthemum.

vivid by far than a list of Latin names are a few delightfully intimate glimpses of how the garden grew, and what grew there, to be found in Augustine Smith's correspondence with his friend, Lady Sophia Tower.

9 May 1850. Scilly is very gay, and still more so could you take a walk in my garden, though the wind has played sad havoc there of late, breaking and shrivelling the ixias, sparaxis, and mesembryanthemums most cruelly: of these last, I have now two of the great large-leaved ones in flower, one being a beautiful yellow, and the other a purple, both as large as Adelaide's face.

13 October 1850. My garden is still in high beauty . . . At present the Guernsey lilies, imported from Mr Luff at Guernsey, are pre-eminent: they are very handsome, but are nothing to the Bella Donnas as to making a show in the garden. I wish I could send you some of my Red Mullet. I have had so many lately that I have hardly known what to do with them, and of enormous size.

'Valhalla' – the museum of figure-heads of some of the many ships wrecked off the rocky coast of Tresco.

'The garden at Tresco is famed throughout the world for rare plants.' A corner of the garden of almost tropical effect.

In the intervals of feasting on mullet and admiring his mesembryanthemums with flowers as large as Adelaide's face (Adelaide must have had a small face, for even in the Isles of Scilly mesembryanthemums seldom show flowers more than four inches across), Augustus Smith found time to represent Truro in the House of Commons. When he died in 1872, an obituary described him as 'a busy, thoughtful and resolute man' which indeed he was. Tireless in his garden-work, thoughtful in devising new methods of cultivating plants and new ways of protecting them from the elements, and resolute in his confidence that he could make a garden on Tresco Island, which had once, to others, seemed so unpromising a prospect.

On the East Rockery, below the house, grow some beautiful ratas from New Zealand (Metrosideros robusta), which are covered with copper-scarlet brushes of flowers in June. Nearby grows a relation of the yucca, Furcraea longaeva, which only flowers after years of preparation, and then rewards its patient cultivator with a spire of creamy green flowers twenty feet high. Echiums, from the Canary Islands, giant cousins of our native anchusa, are a sight at Tresco in spring when they flower in half a dozen dazzling shades of blue. Other plants which grow in very few other British gardens, if any, are the pink-belled correas from Australia, silver pink proteas from South Africa and the violet pea-flowered Podalyria calyptrata from South Africa.

Before leaving this garden of exotics, the visitor must not miss the interesting little museum, 'Valhalla', near the southern entrance of the garden. This contains the figure heads of nearly seventy ships which have been wrecked on the rocky coast of Scilly.

'The influence of the sea is strongly felt at Tresco. It is the sea that brings the Gulf Stream to bless the islands, and make a garden such as Tresco possible . . . it has a radiant climate – a climate which can coax botanical rarities, as well as daffodils, grown by the million for the London market, to take the winds of March with beauty.'

OPEN Monday to Saturday throughout the year: 10 a.m. – 4 p.m. (Closed on Sunday.)
LOCATION (and how to get there) Scilly Isles, by helicopter or boat to St Mary's, thence by small boat to Tresco Island.

STOURHEAD
Wiltshire

Elsewhere in this book it has been stated that the landscape garden is Britain's one great contribution to the world of art. Nowhere is this more vividly illustrated than by the landscape garden at Stourhead.

The house was built and the garden started in 1714 by Henry Hoare, of the well known banking family, but it was his son, also called Henry, who completed the unique garden landscape which we so admire today. Whether the younger Henry had any landscape gardener to help him is uncertain: 'Capability' Brown did not start work on any great scale till 1750, and the celebrated Uvedale Price not until twenty years later. So Stourhead must indeed be the first landscape garden in England.

It has been written,

Henry Hoare must have been a man of outstanding foresight and taste. But to envisage the garden at Stourhead, to imagine the valley filled with water, the bare downs clothed with woods, and the newly created landscape set with temples and grottoes, as in fact Henry Hoare must have done, calls for imaginative and inventive genius of the highest quality. We must remember that in 1740 it had never been done before: 'landscape-gardener' was a term that did not exist, and the romantic, natural garden was as yet unthought of. By damming up two valleys, Henry Hoare created a lake of over twenty acres; the banks he planted with fir and beech trees. Over the year many of the firs have died or been cut down, leaving the beeches to rear their silver trunks in sole splendour. They are now over two hundred years old and in full maturity. Their towering architecture has the effect of making the lakeside banks seem steeper than they are.

Visitors to Stourhead first pass an inn, The Spread Eagle, built two hundred years ago for their accommodation. Suitably refreshed, they make their way towards the lake down a gentle slope: the view from this point at Stourhead must surely be one of the most beautiful man-made perspectives in the world. It might have been conjured or painted by Claude or Poussin; and 'the eye is led away over the water . . . to a succession of further views and vistas, paler and more misty, as they recede. These give the impression of going on, like a dream, for ever.' Such was the art of Henry Hoare.

On their progress round the lake, visitors first pass the Temple of Flora, an elegant building with a pillared and pedimented façade of tawny stone which contrasts well with its leafy background. Later the famous Grotto comes into view, still retaining, 'in this prosaic age, something of the mysterious and romantic atmosphere that it must have had when Pope's celebrated grotto at Twickenham inspired it'.

The Landscape Garden at Stourhead was the first to be made in England.
Work on it was started in the early eighteenth century.

99

ABOVE *An urn of time-worn stone in a flowery setting.*

RIGHT *One of the classical temples which overlook the lake. This one is a replica, though smaller, of the Pantheon in Rome. It was built about 1745 by the architect Henry Flitcroft (1697–1769).*

Steep steps lead down, between moss covered rocks, and the subterranean cavern below is lit, dramatically, by an overhead opening. In an alcove of shells and 'rusticated' stone, John Michael Rysbrack's sculptured nymph reclines on a chilly couch, over which water from a hidden spring perpetually flows. Nearby are inscribed some lines by Pope, a gentle admonition from the sleeping maiden herself:

> Nymph of the grot, these sacred springs I keep
> And to the murmur of these waters sleep.
> Ah, spare my slumbers, gently tread the cave
> And drink in silence, or in silence, lave.

Sparing the nymph's repose, and not pausing to 'lave', the visitor passes quietly on . . . past another statue by Rysbrack, of Neptune with an ever-gushing urn.

Once more in the sunshine, visitors to Stourhead continue round the end of the lake, past a rustic cottage with an inviting seat. From this restful point of vantage, they can admire the lake in all its limpid beauty, its tree-clad banks, and to the right of where they sit, another temple, a smaller replica of the Pantheon in Rome. This was added to the garden in 1745, the year of the last Jacobite rebellion, and has an imposing portico of pillars. Inside there are more statues by Rysbrack, a well-muscled Hercules and a charming figure of Flora. There are also some well executed plaques, in terracotta, of classic scenes.

ABOVE *The Market Cross, far older than the other architectural features at Stourhead, dates from the fourteenth century. It was brought to the garden in 1768 from Bristol, and is one of the best preserved in the country.*

LEFT *The Temple of Flora, with its pillars and pediment.*

The tour continues, and soon yet another temple, the Temple of the Sun, comes into view. This is said to be inspired by the Temple of the Sun at Baalbec. A hundred paces more, and there's the bridge, and the visitors have regained their starting-point.

One more feature remains to be examined; the towering Market Cross which two centuries ago was found in pieces and neglected in a builders yard in Bristol. Henry Hoare brought it to Stourhead, and re-erected it there in its sylvan setting. The cross dates from the early fourteenth century, and in its Anglo-Saxon Gothicry reminds visitors, after the series of classical temples they have just admired, that Stourhead is not in the Campagna, but in England, and in the heart of England too.

OPEN All the year 8 a.m. – 7 p.m. (or sunset, if earlier).
LOCATION At Stourton village on B3092, 3 miles north-west of Mere.

103

3

THE MIDLANDS AND THE NORTH

HOLKER HALL, Cumbria
LEVENS HALL, Cumbria
CHATSWORTH, Derbyshire
HADDON HALL, Derbyshire
BAMPTON MANOR, Oxfordshire
BLENHEIM PALACE, Oxfordshire
PUSEY HOUSE, Oxfordshire
ALTON TOWERS, Staffordshire
NEWBY HALL, Yorkshire
SUTTON PARK, Yorkshire

*Flower beds massed with phlox under the many-windowed
south façade of Holker Hall, built about 1870.*

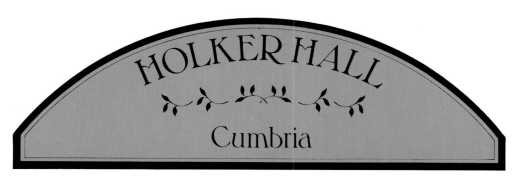

HOLKER HALL
Cumbria

The first owner of Holker Hall who is on record as having taken an interest in the garden is Sir Thomas Lowther, a Member of Parliament, a traveller and, obviously, a man of taste. That was in the eighteenth century. Sir Thomas married a daughter of the Duke of Devonshire, and it was through this marriage that the property came into the family of Mr and Mrs Hugh Cavendish, who live at Holker (pronounced 'Hooker') today.

Sir Thomas bought statues in Italy and brought them to Cumbria by sea, to within a mile of the house, where they were landed at a small, specially built wharf, now long since disappeared. In those spacious days such complicated and expensive operations were more feasible.

The garden at Holker is still shaded by some of the magnificent oaks, beeches and sycamores which Sir Thomas planted – one of the finest cut leaf beeches (Fagus sylvatica heterophylla) in the country grows at Holker – and it is these trees which provide the high shade for the rare rhododendrons, azaleas and magnolias which make the beauty of the garden in spring and summer. The trees have lasted longer than the statues, many of which must have succumbed to the occasional cold Cumbrian winter or have been moved to other Cavendish properties, such as Hardwick, or Chatsworth, described elsewhere in this book. Mr and Mrs Hugh Cavendish hope, in time, to replace them.

The garden at Holker is large, and it is full of surprises: hidden glades, winding paths, with here and there spreading lawns and mossy banks. There are two small formal gardens, one a rose garden, which the visitor approaches through a pergola laden with wistaria, honeysuckle, roses, vines, jasmines, clematis and two unusual climbing plants, Abelia floribunda, from Mexico, with dark red flowers in June, and Schizandra chinensis, from China, with pale pink flowers in spring. The other formally laid out garden consists of herbaceous borders and lies to the south of the new wing of the house, added about 1870. These borders fairly blaze away from mid-May until the first frosts.

But the great beauty of the garden at Holker is the rhododendrons, which revel in the acid soil, the usually mild climate and the site itself of the garden, a slope falling gently to the south, beautifully sheltered and drained – ideal conditions for gardening, and for rhododendrons: there are few months at Holker when there are not some in flower.

Perhaps the rarest rhododendron in the garden is the sweetly scented R. fragrantissimum which flowers there out of doors. It does so in very few English gardens, and even in the benevolent climate of Holker it does not flower every year. First to flower after the very short 'dead' season of October is

Rhododendron nobleanum, which shows its blooms above brown-felted leaves throughout the mild spells of winter. Then Rhododendron praecox, with rosy purple flowers, takes over. After that there is a continuity and generosity of flower, dozens of varieties flowering one after the other, or at the same time, reaching their peak in May, and only ending with the shell-pink-flowered auriculatums in late September. Visitors to Holker often say that they seem to 'see' rhododendrons there for the first time, so at home do they seem, and so much in their natural setting.

The most spectacular moment in the garden is perhaps in May when the towering Rhododendron arboreum are in crimson flower round the fountain.

A fountain throws up its slender jet against a background of scarlet Rhododendron arboreum.

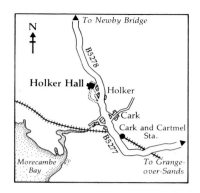

The garden at Holker is at its best in spring – here Rhododendron Loderi (one of the few scented rhododendrons) shows its pink-budded flowers.

These plants, or rather trees, are completely reliable, flowering every year with unfailing regularity and exuberance. They are thought to be over a hundred years old.

Some of the rhododendrons grown at Holker are sweetly scented – Rhododendron ciliatum, especially, with its flowers sometimes showing their rose-red buds through a late fall of snow. In July the Loderi group lays its voluptuous perfume on the air, their pale flowers in sharp contrast with the orange spires of embothrium nearby. Later the flowers of Rhododendron megacalyx scent the air with nutmeg, followed by Rhododendron discolor, one of the hardiest of of the late-flowering rhododendrons from China.

There are many other treats at Holker besides rhododendrons. There is a cherry walk, old mulberry trees, catalpas (Catalpa bignonioides), tulip trees (Liriodendron tulipifera), good specimens of the seldom-grown yellow wood (Cladrastis lutea), Hoheria lyallii from New Zealand, and the rare winter bark (Drymis winteri). Some of these shrubs, planted in the early nineteenth century, are still growing merrily, such as a centagenarian calico bush (Kalmia latifolia): some still carry their original labels, tribute to how carefully the garden has been maintained throughout the years.

A sensational tree in the garden at Holker – sensational in every sense of the word, as will be seen – is a towering Magnolia Campbellii which shows its pink candles of flowers high above the wall lying between the garden and the Ulverston Road. This has sometimes so forcibly caught the eye of passing motorists, that they brake their cars to have another look. Happily, no serious accident has so far resulted.

Another remarkable tree in the garden, though some may think it more curious than beautiful, is a vast monkey puzzle (arucaria), sole survivor of the first batch grown from seed in England by the famous Joseph Paxton, whom we read of elsewhere in connection with the garden at Chatsworth. At the time of the Duke of Devonshire who built a new wing on to the house in the 1870s, this monkey puzzle (already 30 feet high) was blown down and a prize team of shire horses was brought into the garden to heave it into place again: since then it has never looked back. More evidence of how things were easier in those days.

Parts of the garden at Holker may be considered a little informal for some tastes – even a little wild. Wild garlic grows happily among the bluebells, and foxgloves among the rhododendrons. But one guest, many years ago, Lord Robert Cecil, found it very much to his taste, and said it was his idea of the Garden of Eden.

OPEN Easter Sunday – September 30th: daily, except Saturday (special events days excepted) 11 a.m. – 6 p.m.
LOCATION 12 miles from M6 (Exit 36), 4 miles past Grange-over-Sands on B5277 Grange to Newby Bridge road.

LEVENS HALL
Cumbria

The house of Levens, on the green banks of the River Kent in Cumbria, is centuries old, and the present Elizabethan structure replaced an even more ancient building with a peel tower, which was used before 1400 as a fortress against the invading Scots.

At the time of James II and the 'Glorious Revolution' the owner of Levens was James Grahame, a devoted follower of the King and therefore unpopular with the new government when William III succeeded him. Perhaps this, and the lack of money owing to debarment from office, prevented him modernizing the Elizabethan house, which was already somewhat old fashioned. For that we can be grateful. But it did not prevent him planting an elaborate garden. This is the garden we see today – the most famous topiary garden in Britain, and still in perfect shape after nearly three hundred years.

The art of topiary has been a feature of gardens since the earliest times. The word topiary itself derives from the Greek *topos* ('a place'), thus the Latin word *topiarius* came to mean 'the man in charge of the place', or gardener. We are apt to think of topiary as a typically English garden feature, but it was known to the Romans, and Pliny the Younger describes hedges of shorn box in his garden in Tuscany. At the height of the Roman Empire, their subject races emulated everything which was Roman, and clipped shrubs and neatly barboured bay trees were features of the gardens of what is now Turkey and Asia Minor. There are courtyards of clipped myrtle in the Generalife Gardens in Spain, a relic of the Moors who may well have learned the curious art from their Roman overlords. In fact, as we are told that a yew tree takes a thousand years to grow and a thousand years to die, it is possible that somewhere there is an old yew tree still alive in Britain which was once trained by a Roman soldier for his amusement into an amphora, and a thousand years later provided wood for the bows which won the day at Agincourt. And it is not beyond the bounds of possibility that it could be living still, and strong enough to carry a swing for village children today.

Topiary was a feature of Italian and French gardens of the Renaissance, but 'nowhere was it used so spectacularly as it was in English gardens, and topiary, as a garden embellishment, seems as English as the rose'.

However, in popularity, topiary has had its ups and downs. Francis Bacon, in the early sixteenth century was lukewarm about it. 'I for my part', he wrote, 'do not like images cut out in juniper, or other garden stuff: they be for children. But, little low hedges, round like welts, with some pretty pyramids, I like well.' Not everyone would share his qualified enthusiasm.

Yew is a dark and noble tree, and Victoria Sackville-West, whose taste was

The Elizabethan house of Levens is set in a garden of topiary unique in the world.

III

perfect in all gardening matters, describes yew as '. . . grave and masculine' and makes a plea to gardeners to aim at 'heavy and sombre archways, or at huge balls and obelisks': no pretty pyramids for her.

Joseph Addison delivered a scathing attack on the art of topiary in *The Spectator* when he wrote,

Our trees rise in cones, globes and pyramids. We see the mark of scissors upon every plant and bush. I do not know whether I am singular in my opinion, but for my own part, I would rather look upon a tree in all its luxuriancy and diffusion of boughs and branches than when it is thus cut and trimmed into a mathematical figure: and can not but fancy that an orchard in flower looks infinitely more delightful than all the little labyrinths of the most finished parterre.

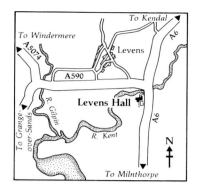

ABOVE *The topiary garden in summer.*

LEFT *Joseph Addison (1672–1719) once wrote 'Our trees rise in cones, globes and pyramids. We see the mark of scissors on every plant and bush . . .' At Levens, the most perfectly preserved of topiary gardens, we still do.*

At about the same time, Richard Steele also poked fun at topiary (then definitely going through one of its unfashionable periods) in a passage which became famous, in which he offered, for imaginary sale,

Adam and Eve in yew: Adam a little shattered by the fall of the tree of knowledge in the great storm: Eve and the Serpent very flourishing.
St George in box: his arms scarce long enough, but will be in a condition to stick the dragon by next April.
A green Dragon of the same, with a tail of ground ivy for the present.
An old Maid of Honour in wormwood.
A quick set Hog, shot up into a porcupine.
A lavender Pig, with sage growing in his belly.

Some years ago I recorded, 'The work of these sharp pens soon swayed the taste of garden owners all over the country . . . the work of sharp axes followed.' Topiary was no longer smart, and splendid gardens of clipped holly and sculptured yew were swept away all over the country. The box hedges at Kensington Palace were uprooted simply because they made Queen Anne sneeze. The new 'Romantic' style won the day – the garden at Levens, mercifully, escaped.

The garden was originally designed for James Grahame by a Frenchman, Beaumont, said to be a pupil of the famous French garden designer, André Le Nôtre, though there is little in his plan for Levens, quite different in scale and feeling, to recall the work of Louis XIV's most famous of all gardeners. However, Monsieur Beaumont certainly worked at Levens, and the gardener's house there is still called Beaumont Hall.

It is the fantastic shapes that the yews and box trees have assumed over the centuries which give the garden at Levens its particular character. Some have their own names – The Great Umbrella, for instance, and Queen Elizabeth and Her Maids of Honour.

Though time has dealt roughly with M. Beaumont's formal plan, and though his trees have, triumphantly, grown out of all proportion to what he originally intended, in part of the garden which the visitor can inspect some semblance of formality survives. Here, south of the Broad Walk, lies an area of nearly 5 acres, lined with imposing beech hedges which give an impression of ordered grandeur of which Le Nôtre would certainly have approved.

But it is the topiary at Levens which make it such an extraordinary creation. It is a truly memorable garden, and in its way, unique.

OPEN Daily: 10 a.m. – 5 p.m, except weekends in the winter.
LOCATION On A6 5 miles south of Kendal, 4 miles from M6 /Exit 36).

CHATSWORTH
Derbyshire

Chatsworth, of the several great houses owned by the Duke of Devonshire, lies in one of the finest and most rugged parts of England. Its very name spells grandeur, and the contents of the house itself, outside the scope of this book, are fabulous. The gardens, in any garden history of England, enjoy an equal fame. Several celebrated garden architects have had a hand in them, and not so many years ago – perhaps seventy-five – an army of eighty gardeners attended to their upkeep; yet, today, with but a handful of gardeners to do the work of that army, the gardens at Chatsworth present as fair a face as ever they did. This has been possible partly as a result of the use of modern methods, certainly, but also, and it is a big also, to the imagination and enthusiasm of the present owners.

Ths history of the gardens at Chatsworth can be approximately divided into five periods. Nothing remains of the Elizabethan garden which, doubtless, once lay beneath the walls of the Tudor house. Of the First Duke's seventeenth-century garden with its elaborate parterres and serried statues, only some fountains, some balustrading and the famous Cascade, one of the sights of Chatsworth, survive. 'Capability' Brown was employed by the Fourth Duke in the eighteenth century to make sweeping changes. The Sixth Duke, born in 1790, restored some of the seventeenth-century formality of the gardens, and made enormous additions of his own, of which more later. In these developments he was aided by the celebrated Joseph Paxton, creator of the Crystal Palace. When the Duke and Paxton had done their work, it has been recorded, 'there ensued a long sunlit century when successive Duchesses loved and nurtured the garden, which grew, under their care and that of countless gardeners, to splendid maturity'. Today, the present ducal couple have devoted imagination and zest to the maintenance of the gardens, and have succeeded in endowing them with new life.

Let us go back to the garden at the time of the First Duke, some of which, as we have seen, still remains. The house, in the late 1600s, was set in a series of terraces, decorated with statues by one of the great sculptors of the day, Caius Cibber. The west parterre, also undertaken at this time, was laid out by George London, partner of Henry Wise, who was afterwards gardener to Queen Anne. He was praised by the diarist John Evelyn for his 'industry, knowledge of nature and genius of soil'.

But the greatest development of the garden in this period resulted from the realization of the existence of the local high-level supply of water, which could make possible the Cascade and fountains that are still the glory of the garden today. These sensational waterworks were the achievement of a Frenchman,

The 'Palace of the Peak', with daffodils
beneath the still leafless trees.

Monsieur Grillet, and were to make the garden famous throughout the land.
Mr Francis Thompson, in his admirable *History of Chatsworth*, has written:

The waterworks were the chief note of the First Duke's garden. Whether in the
form of ponds or of mere fountains, there was water everywhere. The total area of
water, in relation to the size of the whole garden, must have been enormous. Of the
fountains, nine (excluding those connected with the Cascade) are mentioned by name
in the accounts: the Venus Fountain, the Boreas Fountain, the Neptune Fountain, the
Triton Fountain, the Willow Tree Fountain, the Sea Horse Fountain, the fountain in
the new garden (the West parterre) the Greenhouse Fountain; but there were no doubt
many lesser ones. An underground network of pipes and streams survives to this day,
although the fountains themselves have mostly vanished.

But of all the waterworks, the Cascade, completed in 1696, was the most
sensational, and still is.

LEFT *The 'Emperor' fountain at Chatsworth was added to the garden to celebrate a visit from the Tsar of Russia in the early nineteenth century.*

RIGHT *Delphiniums and Iceberg roses, backed with Irish yews in a blue and white border.*

Of all M. Grillet's water toys only the Cascade and the Sea Horse Fountain survive; the quaint Willow Tree Fountain, a copper tree which spouts water over the unwary, is a clever reproduction. As fashion changed, the rest were swept away, though two architectural relics survive from this earlier garden, the great twin pedestals, on the western terrace, surmounted by sphinxes, carved by Cibber.

When Brown had done his work the park at Chatsworth swept right up to the walls of the house. After some initial doubts, that eighteenth-century arbiter of good taste, Horace Walpole, approved, and wrote that he found the garden 'improved by the late Duke, many foolish waterworks being taken away, oaks and rocks being taken into the garden, and a magnificent bridge built'. The bridge, built by James Paine, spans the nearby Derwent river.

No great changes were made in the garden after this for half a century – until the succession of the Sixth Duke in 1811. He was a bachelor, and with no role in public life and no wife to distract him, he devoted his whole life to Chatsworth and, in particular, to its gardens. In 1826 he met Joseph Paxton, and the gardens were never to be the same again. Paxton was of humble origin, but his career was meteoric: as a boy he worked in the Royal Horticulture Society's garden in London for 18s a week; a few years later, after a fortuitous

meeting with the Duke, he was in charge of the Chatsworth gardens, where he built the world's largest greenhouse, and came to be recognized as one of Britain's leading horticulturists; a few more years passed, he built the Crystal Palace and was knighted.

Paxton encouraged the Duke's love of plants, and in the garden at Chatsworth flowerbeds were immensely extended, groves of exotic shrubs planted, and the surrounding hills were clothed with trees. Enormous rocks were moved into the gardens for their romantic and dramatic effect and were given the names of Queen Victoria, Prince Albert and the Duke of Wellington; they are there still. This involved vast expense and labour, but it was nothing to the Duke, who said complacently, 'The spirit of some Druid seems to animate Mr Paxton in these bulky removals.' In comparison, it was the merest child's play to have a Greek column shipped from Greece – the Sunium pillar, still there for all to see.

However, the greatest near-miracle which Paxton conjured at Chatsworth was a vast greenhouse. This, alas, is no more. In its day it was one of the wonders of Britain, and in it the extraordinary Victoria Regia water lily, with leaves 6 feet across and flowers to match, was coaxed into flower in 1838. The greenhouse, or Great Stove as it was then called, was a casualty of the First World War; it had become impossible to heat owing to fuel shortages and most

ABOVE Verbascum raise their yellow candelabra of flowers below a terrace wall.

ABOVE LEFT Rhododendron flowers and the giant leaves of Gunnera manicata, a waterside plant from Brazil, by a rock-face at Chatsworth.

RIGHT Roses in lavender-edged borders by the Orangery.

of its pampered inmates died: so the Ninth Duke decided, somewhat drastically, to blow it up.

From Paxton's day the gardens at Chatsworth changed very little until the last war, when labour problems really became acute. Acres of lawn reverted to rough grass and bedding-out was curtailed. But the splendid overall picture remains surprisingly the same.

The present Duke and Duchess, in spite of all difficulties, have cast a very special spell over their great garden, and some of their additions add a pleasing note of fantasy to the scene. A serpentine hedge undulates towards the Sunium Column. A ground plan of Chiswick Villa, in London, once another Devonshire property, has been traced, in low clipped box, on a lawn, and smaller borders, one in tones of red, orange and gold, and another in Wedgwood shades of blue and white, have been planted near the door to the Statuary Gallery. A new greenhouse, in the most modern taste, houses a collection of exotic plants, while a newly planted maze marks the site of Paxton's Great Stove: this is a special delight for the hundreds of thousands of visitors who come to Chatsworth every year, and, incidentally, substantially contribute to its upkeep.

As the Sixth Duke wrote proudly of his great greenhouse, 'It might well be said of Chatsworth and its garden, they never seem to disappoint anybody, and excite something like enthusiasm in all.'

OPEN March 30th – October 9th (approx): Monday to Friday,
11.30 a.m. – 4.30 p.m. (except Bank Holiday weeks);
Saturday and Sunday, 1.30 p.m. – 5.30 p.m.
Bank Holidays, 11.30 p.m. – 5.30 p.m.
LOCATION On B6012 8 miles north of Matlock.

*The garden was largely reconstructed
in its historic framework in 1912.*

RIGHT *A wall below the top terrace
at Haddon, with a brimming border at*

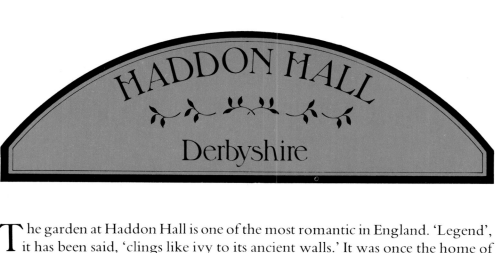

HADDON HALL
Derbyshire

The garden at Haddon Hall is one of the most romantic in England. 'Legend', it has been said, 'clings like ivy to its ancient walls.' It was once the home of Dorothy Vernon, and the story goes that it was from Haddon that Dorothy eloped with her lover, Sir John Manners. The gate through which she ran away, the narrow packbridge which she crossed to meet her waiting lover are still there, and it was certainly through Dorothy Vernon that Haddon came into the Manners family to which it still belongs.

The gardens at Haddon Hall have changed but little since the Vernons' day. They take the form of terraces, each with its own planting scheme, the second and third of which are linked by a magnificent flight of seventy-six steps between a ball-topped balustrade. In summer this balustrade is beautifully wreathed and garlanded with roses. The steps are built of the local stone, and in their construction, so many hundreds of years ago, no mortar was used.

The top terrace, still known as Dorothy Vernon's Walk, was once heavily shaded with great trees, relics of the first planting of the garden when the Ninth Duke of Rutland, head of the Manners family, restored the Hall and garden. These trees, grown somewhat top-heavy, were felled, and in their place a smiling lawn was laid, enlivened by the gay flowerbeds which we see today.

The second terrace, too, was radically altered. This had once been planted with yews, which, when originally set out, were kept quite small and clipped,

its foot, and roses above. In the border are verbascums and heleniums.

in the fashion of the day, into balls, obelisks and peacocks. Over the years when Haddon Hall was unoccupied, the garden was allowed to fall into neglect, and the yews, untroubled by the gardeners' shears, romped away and became full-grown trees. These too were cleared away, and more lawn took their place, edged with new, small topiary trees which are rigorously kept in shape.

Few gardens still exist of which all the main features – steps, paving, balustrading – are over three hundred years old. But if the framework of the garden at Haddon is ancient, the planting is modern, with a strong accent on floribunda roses.

RIGHT *Peverell's Tower, seen over white roses on the topmost terrace of the garden at Haddon.*

BELOW *The lowest terrace is composed of lawn, and the famous garden steps (dating from Dorothy Vernon's day) lead down to it. The stair has seventy six steps, of stone, but without mortar.*

The planting of any garden changes from year to year, otherwise it would become lifeless and static. It is probable that, since the writer's last visit to Haddon, some of the roses may have been replaced by others, but he remembers a shining mass of the golden-flowered floribunda rose, Chinatown, and an imposing group of the deep crimson, strongly scented Papa Meilland. Other roses which enriched the over-all tapestry of colour were light pink Poulsens, deep red Frensham, and the new charming, pale pink Dearest.

The walls of the terraces of Haddon are hung with roses, too, as well as with clematis and vines: climbing roses such as the wine-dark Clos Vougeot, the pale, late-flowering New Dawn and the popular Albertine of the bright coral buds.

A great connoisseur of gardens and well known garden writer, Mr A. G. L. Hellyer, once wrote, 'such is Haddon Hall, a place of dreams, and a garden of exquisite beauty. It would be a dull visitor indeed whose imagination was not struck by it.'

OPEN April 1st – September 30th: Tuesday – Saturday, 11 a.m. – 6 p.m. (closed Sundays and Monday).
LOCATION Off A6 between Bakewell and Rowsley.

123

Good taste is a quality which is difficult to achieve, and not easy to define – but in the garden at Bampton Manor the good taste of the owner, Countess Münster, is everywhere apparent. And the garden owner who wants to improve his own blessed plot will come away full of ideas as to how to do it, new ideas for planting plans – new and telling juxtapositions of plants – and for plants themselves.

For example, almost every garden, in the spring, has a show of wallflowers. These are a tradition in British gardens, and, incidentally, the envy of American gardeners, as they do not prosper in America, where the winters are too cold for them. But the wallflowers most British gardeners plant, are usually the traditional brown or yellow, or occasionally a 'Persian carpet' mixture of different colours, and very effective and pretty they are. At Bampton Manor, however, more thought has been given to the choice of the original seed packets; and the wallflowers there are in colours which, in their novelty, surprise and delight the eye – pink, rose-coloured, and pale lemon-yellow. That is only one example of how the garden at Bampton Manor is planted with just that subtle difference which is the evidence of taste.

Bampton Manor and its garden lie almost completely surrounded by the pretty old village of Bampton, and presiding proudly over the garden scene is a feature which is well outside the garden walls, the slim fifteenth-century spire of St Mary's Church. Most fortunately placed, the spire can be seen from almost every angle of the garden, and acts as what in the eighteenth century was called an eye-catcher. No garden could have a more effective one.

The garden at Bampton Manor is divided into sections, each with its own colour scheme and its own character. The expectant visitor, on arrival at the gate, walks up a short drive, with a miniature lake to his right. In spring this is surrounded with early iris and the clear gold flowers of king cups (Caltha palustris), and in summer with the jungly vegetation of giant rhubarbs (Rheum atropurpureum), rodgersias, Saxifraga peltata, and other plants to provide a lush and exotic effect. Red and white water lilies float on the water's surface, and a willow weeps the days away by the water's edge.

From the drive, to the left, the tall trees are underplanted in spring with daffodils and a myriad of scarlet tulips, which grow happily in the grass, showing their flowers year after year. Beyond lies a circular white garden planted only with white flowers and shrubs, including willow-leaved pear (Pyrus salicifolia), with silver foliage. In the centre of this round enslosure, of which the walls are of closely clipped yew, a perfect background for white flowers, is an elegant white temple of wire, curtained in summer with white clematis

RIGHT *Beyond a neatly-laid terrace of stone and pebbles, are twin trees of the fastigiate cherry P. serrulata erecta – in Japanese Amanogawa.*

BELOW *An urn makes a focal point in a close-hedged garden of striped tulips.*

Marie Boisselot, and underplanted, in the crevices of the paving, with the unusual white willow herb, Epilobium glabellum.

Near the Manor itself are twin herbaceous borders which make a fine show from May till the first frosts. Here, as everywhere in the garden, taste and knowledge of plants have been shown in the planting – pink bergamot, tobacco flowers, gypsophila Bristol Fairy, white and blue galega, verbascum Pink Domino and many other favourite flowers make a haze of gentle colour for months on end. These borders are on the exact axis between the front door of the Manor with its Gothick porch, and the church spire. They have been described by experts as among the best herbaceous borders in the country.

Passing down the broad grass path between them, the visitor reaches an open area, planted round the edge with loosely grouped shrubs, the best varieties of each, among which are the spreading Eupatorium ligustrinum, Hypericum

Elstead, mock orange (Philadelphus microphyllus) and the crimson-budded rock rose, Cistus corbariensis. Nearer at hand are a group of old shrub roses, which, growing in rough grass, have made fine plants 8 or 10 feet high and are laden with flowers in June and July. Among the finest specimens are handsome bushes of Fantin Latour, Rosa mundi, Charles de Mills, Tuscany and Tour de Malakoff.

There is another part of the garden at Bampton devoted, in the main, to roses. This lies under the classical east façade of the Manor itself . . . but it is a rose garden with a difference. Roses there are in abundance, both hybrid teas in bush form and grown as standards. But the difference lies in the fact that they are underplanted with silver and grey aromatic plants which give the garden a uniquely rich, upholstered look – and do away with those areas of bare earth which disfigure so many rose gardens. The ground-covering and,

127

*Wistaria curtains the Gothick facade
of Bampton Manor in May.*

RIGHT *A woodland walk is close-carpeted
with polyanthus and scillas.*

incidentally, weed-suppressing, plants used to achieve this effect are silver and gold thymes, santolina (the white leaved lavender cotton), senecio (well named greyii for its leaves are the colour and texture of grey velvet), phlomis, and for some muted colour, the mat-forming campanulas. The rose garden at Bampton Manor is as successful a conception as can be seen in the length and breadth of Britain.

There is another aspect of the garden at Bampton Manor which is worth recording, and which makes it doubly interesting to the garden visitor. Often, while visiting famous gardens, the visitor sees plants he would like to have himself. But if they are unusual varieties (as many of the plants at Bampton are) he is posed with the problem of where to get them. At Bampton the answer, nine times out of ten, is, 'Just through the gate into the kitchen garden,' for it is here that Countess Münster raises, grows and sells many of the most effective plants in her garden.

So the visitor to the garden at Bampton Manor comes away, not only with some envy in his heart and some new ideas in the back of his mind, but also with some of the plants he most admired in the back of his car.

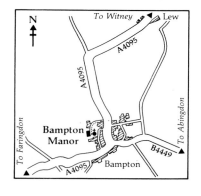

OPEN Weekdays for sale of plants and on several other days every summer for special charities.
LOCATION Entrance gates on left of Bampton to Witney road leaving Bampton village.

BLENHEIM PALACE
Oxfordshire

The visitor to the gardens at Blenheim Palace, should look for four things. First, the surrounding park, surely 'Capability' Brown's masterpiece. Second, the bridge, over which there has always been such controversy, and under which, at times, so little water. Third, the Edwardian terrace-garden, legacy of a Vanderbilt Duchess sixty years ago. Fourth? This is a feature of the gardens at Blenheim which all but the most knowing garden visitor might overlook – the spring woodland garden created in the last twenty years by the late Duke of Marlborough. Quite small, and all but lost in the vast pleasure grounds which surround it, this little garden is easily missed, but is one of the most delightful and human corners of the whole garden. Each of these four features will be dealt with in turn.

The story of Blenheim Palace itself is well known. How a grateful Queen Anne offered her victorious general – the first Duke of Marlborough – the royal domain of Woodstock; how she promised to build him a suitable palace there; how this, in course of time, was done by the most brilliant and talented architect of the day, Sir John Vanbrugh; how troubles followed, when the Marlboroughs fell from favour, and how, finally, the Duke himself had to complete his great house and gardens at his own expense. The story is in every guide book: our task is to describe the grounds and gardens, their construction and creation; and how they impress a visitor to Blenheim today.

The park at Blenheim, as previously mentioned, is often thought of as 'Capability' Brown's finest work: his creation of the lake, by damming the meandering River Glyme, has been acclaimed by that great authority, Sacheverell Sitwell as the 'one great argument for the landscape gardener – there is nothing finer in Europe'. The park itself is a thing of perpetual beauty, and is an example of Brown's work at its best. It has been often said that the one great British contribution to art is the idea of the landscape garden. No foreign country, though they have tried, has ever succeeded in planting anything remotely similar. 'They stand alone . . . green misty perspectives such as Claude painted, but his countrymen were quite incapable of planting; dreamy opalescent distances, sometimes peopled by deer, but more often by cows, for this is England, not Arcadia.' The park at Blenheim is one of these inspired creations.

The second feature of the grounds at Blenheim, which it was suggested the visitor should examine, is Vanbrugh's bridge, if only on account of the trouble it caused from its very inception. Vanbrugh had set his heart on an imposing bridge to act as approach to his brand new palace. But it had to be a bridge of some importance to be in keeping with the grandeur of the building.

Lupins make a bright foreground for
the imposing towers of Vanbrugh's Palace.

131

Unfortunately a bridge has to cross something – a valley, a ravine, or more usually a river. The land round the new palace was undulating – nothing more: and the River Glyme was only a sleepy, rush-bordered stream. But Vanbrugh had his way, and his bridge was built, and so large was it that it was possible to accommodate dwellings, each with several rooms, in its giant fabric. Frantic efforts were made, by canalization, to increase the flow of the inadequate Glyme, to give the bridge more water to span, but without success. It was not until 1764, long after the death of Blenheim's first occupants, that 'Capability' came on the scene – and transformed it. He changed the Glyme, by damming, into a serpentine lake, which had all the appearance of a river. This was such a success that he joked that he doubted whether the Thames would ever forgive him. In the process, some of the built-in living rooms were flooded, but that could not be helped; and it is doubtful if the dwellings were ever meant for human habitation. That is the story of Vanbrugh's bridge over Brown's lake at Blenheim: one of the classic stories in the history of British landscape gardening.

The third feature of the gardens at Blenheim that takes and holds the eye of the visitor is the Baroque terraces lying to the west of the Palace, running down towards the lake. These were an addition to the garden made by the Ninth Duke, who married the beautiful and enormously rich Consuelo Vanderbilt. Vanbrugh, aided by Henry Wise, had created a formal garden at Blenheim which was one of the sights of England. 'Capability' Brown, with his passion for the natural look in gardens, swept them away. The Ninth Duke did his best, with the aid of a French garden architect, Achille Duchêne, to put them back. And there they are today – not quite as Vanbrugh's were, but elaborate and grandiose enough for any palace. If they have a slightly exotic and un-English look, they are none the less impressive for that. And with the parterres ablaze with bedded out plants in summer, and the black and gilded fountains playing, they make as brave a show as can be seen on this side of the Channel.

Before leaving the marvels of the terraces and park, before blinking, for the last time, at Vanbrugh's jumbo bridge, the visitor must seek the fourth feature

A new formal garden, with spectacular fountains, was laid out by the French garden architect Achille Duchêne, for the ninth Duke, in 1925.

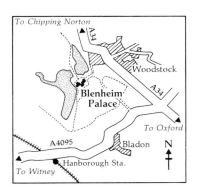

ABOVE *Lancelot 'Capability' Brown, in 1764, gave Vanbrugh's too massive bridge 'something worth crossing', by damming the little river Glyme to make a lake.*

ABOVE RIGHT *The view westward towards the lake, over Duchêne's baroque water garden.*

of the garden at Blenheim – the secret Spring Garden which was the late Duke's special joy. It is in sharp, but perhaps comforting, contrast to Vanbrugh's theatrical and massive architecture, Brown's misty perspectives and Duchêne's stylish terraces. A little garden, hidden in the trees, it exhibits the 'taste in gardening as understood in the twentieth century'. Winding paths lead between banks of small trees and shrubs, which though they are at their best in spring and early summer, show pleasing vistas of flowers and contrasting leaves until the first frosts. Here are rare species hydrangeas, glaucous-leaved hostas, blue Tibetan poppies. And in specially prepared beds of acid soil (necessary in most parts of Oxfordshire), there are many-coloured rhododendrons and azaleas.

Such is the garden at Blenheim. And in this short account much has been left out: the Cascade in the park, devised by 'Capability' Brown in 1764; the Kitchen Garden, with its walls like the bastions of a fortress; the two mighty avenues, planted on military lines; the Great Avenue and the Mall; and one last but charming detail – an eighteenth-century sphinx on one of the terraces, which proudly carries a portrait head of the beautiful American wife of the Ninth Duke.

OPEN March 1st – October 31st: 11.30 a.m. – 5 p.m.
LOCATION Off A34, 8 miles north of Oxford.

133

PUSEY HOUSE
Oxfordshire

The garden at Pusey House, near Faringdon, with its long view over the lake towards the White Horse Hill of Uffington, has been largely created in the last forty-five years by the present owners, Mr and Mrs Michael Hornby.

On arrival at Pusey the visitor enters through a side gate which gives on to a path, planted on either side with richly coloured borders. The border on the left conceals the tennis court; the one on the right, the kitchen garden. These twin borders are thickly planted with all the most colourful of flowers, interspersed with Iceberg roses, and backed by the giant Scottish thistles (Onopordon arabicum) and towering cardoon artichokes. These touches of silver serve effectively to set off the more vivid flowers, and the borders make a heartwarming welcome to the garden. At the end of the path is a gate of airy ironwork, painted, the better to set it off, a subtle shade of grey, and bearing a shield with the Hornby arms. Through this gate the full panorama of the garden at Pusey is revealed: the lake, the spreading lawns, and to right and left the main herbaceous border, over 150 yards long and one of the most impressive in England.

It is a border planted with an overall idea, an overall colour scheme, and its plan comprises all the flowers which one would expect to find in a well planted border of the 1970s. Blue seems to be the predominant colour – the different blues of delphiniums, of Salvia superba, of galega, and of nepeta. But, in the popular taste of the day, the main colour is sparked with the occasional splash of silver leaves, and softened with soft pinks, and light and darker mauves.

At this point the visitors to Pusey are offered a choice of routes: to the right or left? Their curiosity to see the house itself will probably suggest a turn to the left, down a broad gravel path, with the border, a bright galaxy of flowers, on one side, and a green lawn, sloping down to the lake, on the other. Soon the eighteenth-century house comes into view, and its south facade, said to be the work of the architect, John Wood of Bath, can be admired.

When Mr and Mrs Hornby first came to Pusey, the lawn swept up to the walls of the house in the classical style approved by 'Capability' Brown. One of their first changes was to add the wide terrace of grey stone, designed by the well known architect Mr Geoffrey Jellicoe. This broad expanse of stonework, facing south and warmed by any sun that is going, might have seemed somewhat daunting had it not soon been softened by plantings of creeping plants, and cushioned by twin clumps of that grey, velvet-leaved shrub Jerusalem sage (Phlomis fruticosa). On either side of its steps are stone boxes usually planted every summer with scented-leaved geraniums.

Leaving the terrace on the left, the path continues towards a corner of the

The 'Chinese' bridge 'elegantly spans the lake only a foot above the water'. It was added to the garden in about 1745. In the foreground, a brightly flowered clump of Lysimachia punctata.

garden planted primarily with the 'old-fashioned' roses which are so popular today. Here are roses such as the vigorous, pale pink Fantin Latour, the heavily scented Louise Odier, Madame Calvat with its coral flowers and red-tinged leaves, and one of the best of all roses, with flowers as furbelowed as peonies, Paul Neyron. A step or two further on and a spreading group of the hybrid musk rose, Penelope, scents the whole area around it.

Now, another almost unique feature of the garden at Pusey comes into view – the bridge, which has elegantly spanned the lake for more than two centuries since 1755. It is Oriental in inspiration, with its Chinoiserie railings and decorative finials; its low horizontal lines and crisp white paintwork make it particularly pleasing to the eye.

Over the bridge on the further bank the way lies to the left, past a waterside planting of primulas, gold-flowered clumps of the loosestrife Lysimachia

ABOVE *Regale lilies like to grow with their heads in the sun and their roots shaded.*

LEFT *In a walled garden called 'Lady Emily's' there are formal rose beds, but Verbascum bombyciferum is allowed to seed itself where it chooses.*

punctata, and bold groups of hostas. These, like euphorbias, enjoy greater popularity today than ever before. There seems to be something about their blue-green glaucous leaves which modern garden-makers find especially satisfying: their foliage is striking from early spring till late summer, whether it is H. glauca which is planted, or H. marginata, with its white edged leaves, or the gold-splashed variety, H. variegata. Though the flowers of hostas, or plantain lilies, are comparatively uninteresting, their splendid leaves rightly win them a place in every connoisseur's garden. Nearby, at Pusey, grows another popular plant of today, a plant which is a great favourite of flower arrangers, Alchemilla mollis. The flowers of ladies' mantle are a pale but vivid green and its leaves are dressed with silky hairs which take raindrops and hold them like jewels long after the shower is past.

Leaving the lakeside behind, the visitor comes to an area planted with flowering shrubs and rare trees. Fine specimens are on every hand, and to mention just a few, there is a giant Hydrangea villosa, a fine broom (Cytisus battandieri), a North American flowering dogwood (Cornus nuttali), and a stranvaesia. Another most effective planting is of Rhus cotinus, the purple-leaved variety of sumach, against a backing of the silver-leaved willow pear (Pyrus salicifolia), one of the best of all grey-leaved trees, with groups of Deutzia rosea at the sides. It is juxtapositions such as these, which only thought and knowledge could have brought about, which make the garden at Pusey and Mr and Mrs Hornby's achievement there so remarkable. In this part, too, there are several interesting trees: good specimens of liquidambar, the autumn-colouring Cercidiphyllum japonicum, paperbark maple (Acer griseum), and the lovely and too seldom planted yellow-flowered cherry, Prunus Ukon.

Before long, the visitor to Pusey emerges on to a wide swathe of lawn, with a good view to his right over the lake towards the house. In a bed on one side, Mr and Mrs Hornby have lately planted many attractive shrubs which have quickly settled down in their new quarters, making a wide tapestry of leaf and flower. Here grow so many shrubs, roses and trees that to enumerate more than just a few would make tedious reading. Outstanding are some philadelphus (P. aureus) of the golden leaves, the purple-eyed Belle Etoile, the pure white Virginal and the aptly-named Manteau d'Hermine. Nearby are several unusual and rather tender shrubs which deserve mention: Indigofera geraldiana, the pink indigo plant, Rubus Tridel and the little-grown Lespedeza Thunbergii. Some of the trees are of great distinction. There are good maples, such as Acer drummondii, laxiflorum and capillipes, and some impressive members of the sorbus family, notably S. Mitchellii with its large grey leaves. To return to the house, the visitor must make his way under some venerable trees, where in spring the ground is thick with daffodils, snowdrops and periwinkles. Another bridge, of plainer design, crosses the narrow end of the lake, and on the other side the visitor comes on a temple of grey stone with an oddly Oriental dome.

Not far from here lies Lady Emily's Garden, named after Lady Emily Herbert who married Philip Bouverie Pusey, then owner of Pusey, in 1822. It is a small secluded garden, planted in the main with roses, silver Artemisia palmeri and here and there the white, woolly-leaved Verbascum bombyciferum. The walls around are wreathed in more roses, Albertine, Alberic Barbier, Lady Waterlow and New Dawn, with here and there white clematis and the huge velvety leaves of Hydrangea sargentiana. As the visitor leaves this garden,

137

ABOVE *A Victorian figure, in terra-cotta, curtained with musk roses.*

RIGHT *A gate of airy wrought iron, painted a subtle shade of pale blue, which shows up the fine tracery, and complements the flower-colour around.*

reluctantly, for it casts a kind of spell, he admires a bold group of Achillea Golden Plate lifting their flat yellow faces to the sun. The way lies to the left, by the side of the great herbaceous border, and before long the visitor finds himself once more at the wrought iron gate, through which the main garden at Pusey was originally entered, and the visit is over. But whoever comes to Pusey might do well to pause at this point, and look back across the lake and towards the Chinese bridge: the scene is an idyllic one, with a pictorial serenity all its own.

OPEN April 3rd – July 3rd (approx): Wednesday, Thursday, Sunday, 2 p.m. – 6 p.m.
July 5th – October 16th (approx): daily (except Monday and Friday), 2 p.m. – 6 p.m.
Bank Holiday weekends and Mondays: 2 p.m. – 6 p.m.
LOCATION On B4508 between Faringdon and Oxford.

ALTON TOWERS
Staffordshire

LEFT *The Chinese Pagoda, set in the middle of a small lake, with ducks. It was designed by Robert Abraham (1774–1850) for the 15th Earl of Shrewsbury in 1824.*

BELOW *The flower-filled terraces are bright with roses and other flowers all summer.*

Alton Towers lies nearly midway between Ashbourne and Cheadle, in the picturesque valley of the river Churnet.

The creator of the magnificent gardens that the visitor to Alton sees today was the Roman Catholic Charles, Fifteenth Earl of Shrewsbury, who succeeded to the title in 1786. He was then thirty-four, a man 'of a very retired temper and much addicted to music and mechanics'. At that time the chief Shrewsbury home was not at Alton, but at Heythrop in Oxfordshire. All there was at Alton was a simple house called Alveton Lodge described as 'a comfortable homestead, with farm buildings adjoining'. It was surrounded by poor farm land, bare rocks, and hills; and it was overrun with rabbits.

Lord and Lady Shrewsbury were a childless couple, and only visited Alton occasionally. It was not until Lord Shrewsbury was in his sixtieth year that he decided to 'exercise his imagination and talent for landscape design on the bare and rocky hillsides of the Churnet valley'. In 1812 a nearby hill and the grounds adjoining it were enclosed, and two years later Lord Shrewsbury moved into Alveton Lodge, so that he could keep a personal eye on the work to be done, and personally supervise the conjuring, out of wild and desolate scenery, of the beautiful, romantic and picturesque landscape that Alton presents today.

Fortunately Lord Shrewsbury was immensely rich, and had at his command the limitless resources which he needed for his grandiose plans. Labourers, builders, masons and an army of gardeners were brought in to carve out terraces, delve valleys and lay out the gardens. Thousands of tons of soil were excavated to make pools and canals. Water was laid on from a spring two miles away. At the waving of Lord Shrewsbury's golden wand, paths meandered in every direction, fountains threw up their crystal water-drops, and staircases clambered up and down the slopes.

A feature today, as it was early in the last century, is the architecture of the garden at Alton. This includes the Chinese Pagoda fountain, designed by Robert Abraham, with its 70-foot plume of water soaring above the treetops, and the Gothic Temple made of cast iron, a new material in those days. From this point of vantage the whole astonishing panorama of the Alton garden can still be admired. There was, and is, a Swiss Cottage which was the home of a blind Welsh Harper, whose duty it was to 'discourse the music of his distant hills' and fill the valley with melody for the delight of the family and visitors of the Earl, as they strolled among the beauties of the gardens.

Meanwhile, as the gardens grew in beauty, with some assistance from the architect Augustus Pugin, so did the 'comfortable homestead' of Alveton Lodge. Simple dwelling no longer, it sprouted Gothic pinnacles and battlements. To suit its new grandeur it was renamed Alton Abbey, though it was never to know an abbot or a monk.

Charles, Earl of Shrewsbury, died in 1827 and was succeeded by his nephew John, 'the good Earl', who, when the family seat at Heythorp was burned down, made his home at Alton and added to it still further. Once more it changed its name and became Alton Towers. The gardens were extended and brought to further perfection.

Near the Chapel, 'Her Ladyship's Garden' was lovingly laid out. This nestles between two wings of the main house and is a garden of roses in a setting of magnolias and rhododendrons, a place of great beauty in high summer.

On their way to the great Conservatory (also designed by Abraham), now beautifully restored, visitors to Alton pass the Dutch Garden, with its guardian lions. Nearby they pause to admire the Choragic Monument which the filial Earl John put up in memory of his father, the creator of the garden at Alton. The monument, in the Corinthian style, is a replica of the monument to Lysicrates erected in Athens in 344 BC (Choragus means 'the leader of a chorus'). On its walls are inscribed the apt words 'He made the desert smile'.

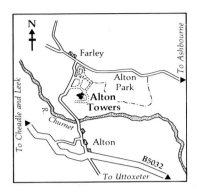

RIGHT *The Choragic Monument, built by 'the filial Earl John, in memory of his father', who created the splendid garden at Alton Towers.*

BELOW *The rock garden is full of colour in July when the spiraeas are in pink and scarlet flower.*

And here might be the moment to pause in our admiration of the gardens at Alton, to insert an irreverent aside. It must be remembered that when Lord Shrewsbury was scattering his temples and pagodas about his unkempt Staffordshire valley, his trees and shrubs had not grown up to create a leafy setting for them, and soften the general outline. His 'follies', in the early days of their existence, may have struck an incongruous, if not faintly ridiculous, note. His son had dutifully inscribed, 'He made the desert smile', but a local wit added, '. . . and a polite desert it was, not to laugh outright'. But we must be respectful.

Below the Choragic Monument, the rock garden sweeps down a slope, as colourful as a peacock's tail. This is spectacular all through the spring and summer, but never more so than in July when the thousands of spiraeas with which it is planted are in flower.

The gardens at Alton Towers are famous for their architectural features which now, embowered by full grown trees, seem an integral part of the Staffordshire scene. They are also renowned for their rhododendrons and rare trees. A choice few of these would include the graceful tulip tree (Liriodendron tulipifera), the incense cedar (Calocedrus decurrens), the fern leaved beech (Fagus sylvatica), and some fine Judas trees (Cercis siliquastrum).

To have conjured, from barren wasteland, the enchanted, almost fairytale gardens at Alton is a rare achievement. It would be quite impossible today. And the thousands of visitors who come to Alton every year should spare a grateful thought for the maker of this magical demesne. Charles Talbot, Earl of Shrewsbury, who indeed created beauty, sparked with fantasy, where nothing was before.

OPEN Good Friday – first weekend in October: 9.30 a.m. – dusk.
LOCATION Situated in triangle between Leek, Ashbourne and Uttoxeter.
All approach roads are signposted.

143

NEWBY HALL
Yorkshire

Yorkshire is a county of great gardens, and one of the most celebrated is the garden at Newby Hall.

The late Major Compton, father of the present owner, inherited house and garden in 1925. The garden looked very different then, and he soon set about improving it. At that time, he wrote,

. . . a number of paths wandered pointlessly through rough grass. There was a period-piece rock garden designed by Miss Ellen Wilmott (of garden fame) and a Victorian parterre on both south and west fronts. I was determined, in those early days, to make a garden worthy of the beautiful house, and I soon realized that to enable me to do so, I would have to have shelter, as the whole 25 acres were very wind-swept. I planned the garden on a central axis, which seemed the obvious thing to do. This axis sloped from the house down to the river some 350 yards away, and to form the axis itself I extended the existing short double borders so that they ran the whole length from the upper terraces down to the river, and backed them with walls of yew. The rest of the garden I built round this axis and the few existing trees, so that by degrees the individual gardens planned themselves, so to speak. In this I was much influenced by Lawrence Johnson's garden at Hidcote of which I was a great admirer (see page 81). The Victorian parterres were replaced by plain lawns and flagstone walks, and Miss Wilmott's large rock garden was joined up to the rest of the garden by suitable paths . . . Further features were added, and the original shelter belts were either thinned or had vistas cut through them. I think at the back of my mind I wanted each self-contained garden to represent a certain picture at a certain time of the year; for instance, one enclosure is called the 'Autumn Garden', another the 'Species Rose Garden', and others . . . 'Sunk Garden', 'Blue and Yellow Garden', and so on. The target to be aimed at seemed to me to be (a) privacy and shelter and (b) sound architectural construction, both of these to my mind being of greater importance than mere colour itself. In many ways one can better appreciate a garden by viewing it in winter rather than in summer.

Background, again, is important. Take, for example, roses. So much of their beauty lies in their foliage, so admirably designed to set off flowers. This foliage beauty is so often lost by surrounding the roses with grass and greenery. At Newby we tried the experiment of a sunk garden with flagstones, and a surround of copper beech – a perfect foil for the delicate foliage and lovely flowers of the rose.

As Major Compton described, the garden at Newby is laid out on a gentle slope down to the River Ure, to the south. The main plan of the garden is a simple one, and is built round the two main axes: the north–south axis which consists of a wide grass path backed by yew hedges running down towards the river, as already described, and the east–west axis, which takes the form of a wide gravelled path known as the Statue Walk. These two main paths are very

*A broad grass walk leads up to the house between
borders of shrubs and herbaceous plants.*

different in character – the grass path is enclosed on either side by broad and generously planned herbaceous borders, while the east–west gravel path is quite different: a broad terrace simply but impressively planted on one side with a formal combination of Irish yew, Cotoneaster horizontalis and purple-leaved Prunus Pissardii. This planting, which otherwise might have made an almost sombre impression, is effectively enlivened by a group of statues from Italy – a little the worse for wear, thanks to many Yorkshire winters, but still graceful and evocative: the pale pearly grey of their worn stone contrasts most effectively with the colouring of their setting, the dark green of the yews, the

The sunk garden at Newby is closely-planted, not only with seasonal flowers, but with permanent low-growing evergreens. (such as ericas and Viburnum Davidii.)

RIGHT *A balustraded corner of the garden with a planting sparked with the silver of* Cineraria maritima. *Beyond lies the lily pond.*

BELOW *To be fully effective flower-borders should be wide and have a background, as here. Boldly planted mixed groups of red and yellow dahlias.*

white flowers and red berries, in turn, of the cotoneaster, and the darker red of the prunus.

The herbaceous borders on the north–south axis are planted, as all such borders should be, with large groups of herbaceous plants, interspersed at intervals with flowers of short season. Clumps of wallflowers, forget-me-nots and tulips being succeeded by antirrhinums and geraniums as the summer advances. Besides the more usual plants to be found in an herbaceous border, there are several in the planting scheme at Newby which specially take the eye, and often invite enquiries: plants such as the unusual Veratrum nigrum, with its deeply ribbed leaves and wine-red flowers; the giant-leaved seakale (Crambe orientalis) with its cloud of tiny white flowers; and several good artemisias such as ludoviciana and Silver Queen, more satisfactory plants than the more usual – and more invasive – A. palmeri. For form, and lasting architectural effect, some shrubs are included in the borders at Newby. These are chosen for their light and graceful habit, rather than for their bulk, for Major Compton thought that such shrubs consort best with the delicate structure and flowers of herbaceous plants. Among these carefully chosen shrubs are Rosa rubrifolia, described earlier, the airy Cytisus aetnensis which casts so light a shade that plants can be safely set beneath it, and Weigela florida foliis purpureis, a pink-flowered, purple-leaved weigela of particularly elegant carriage.

Another delightful part of the garden at Newby is called 'Sylvia's Garden' after Major Compton's late wife. This is a sunk parterre, partially shaded by a giant cedar tree. Here grow all Sylvia Compton's favourite plants, and the stone paths are bordered with fragrant cushions of pinks, aubretia, thymes and nepeta. The height of the planting is carefully kept low, to maintain a carpet effect; and the highest plants are lavender and spreading santolina. An exception is made for regale lilies, which, for a few weeks in late summer, are to be seen with their fragrant white trumpets blowing above the over-all haze of pale blue and mauve.

The visitor to this northern garden who has a taste for 'new' plants will be gratified by the number of new acquaintances in the plant world he will make at Newby. And the writer remembers meeting there, for the first time, several

ABOVE *Brightly planted borders line a path leading to the house.*

LEFT *The great value in any garden of plants and trees of coloured foliage is demonstrated by this lavish use of red-leaved Prunus pissardii and Copper beech (Fagus sylvatica cuprea).*

plants which have remained his staunch friends ever since – Euphorbia wulfenii, for instance, the noblest of all spurges; Pyrus salicifolia, the silver pear, a shapely, small tree; Photinia fruticosa (of which the form Red Robin is outstanding); and the best of all Pampas grasses, Cortaderia bertinii. All friends made at Newby.

'Meeting' plants in other peoples' gardens, making friends with them, so that from then on you either grow them yourself, or greet them as friends when you see them elsewhere, is surely one of the great pleasures of gardening.

OPEN Easter Saturday – second Sunday in October: Monday, Tuesday, Friday 11 a.m. – 6.30 p.m. Wednesday, Thursday, Saturday: 2 p.m. – 6.30 p.m. Sundays, Bank Holiday Mondays and Tuesdays: 11 a.m. – 6.30 p.m.
LOCATION B6265 Ripon to Boroughbridge road. Turn right to Skelton after crossing River Ure. Proceed for 200 yards, then signposted. If coming from Boroughbridge turn off old A1 on leaving town, proceed 3 miles, then signposted.

149

*A rose–hung temple of airy wirework with an iron statue to the right. On the brick wall
are to be seen the starry yellow flowers of Potentilla arbusculus.*

SUTTON PARK
Yorkshire

S utton Park is situated eight miles north of York. It is a classically built house dating from 1747. To the south lies the garden, of which the main features are three wide terraces, two of them planted with overflowing borders. The third has, for a centre piece, a spacious lily pond.

Though open to the public for many months every year, the garden at Sutton Park is very personal, and has been made in the last twenty years by its owners, the late Major Reginald Sheffield and his wife.

Let us visit the garden terrace by terrace. The upper terrace is largely paved to provide a sitting-out area to the house, the walls of which are hung with roses and clematis. One clematis, in particular, is spectacular in late summer, the white, foamy-flowered Clematis recta. To left and right on the upper terrace, and sheltered by the house walls, are two borders which could well merit the expressive French phrase '*parterres précieux*'. These twin borders are planted with carefully chosen plants, some quite rare, such as unusual euphorbias, artemisias, oregan, and the exotic and seldom grown tigridia. The paving of the terrace itself is set with low mat-forming plants, long suffering – or masochistic? – things such as gold and silver aromatic thymes, jade leaved acaenas and velvety stachys. Here and there, making effective exclamation marks, are tufts of the Satin Iris (Sisyrinchium striatum), from Chile.

On the far side of the top terrace and opposite the house, is a fully planted border with standard roses and wistarias to give height, and clumps of green tobacco flowers and claret-leaved perillas to provide some exotic notes of colour. Steps, flanked on either side by terracotta bowls of mixed geraniums, lead down to the second terrace and the rose garden.

RIGHT *Lilies and lavender against a background of cedars.*

The rose garden at Sutton Park is considered to be one of the best designed in England and the original plan was devised by the eminent garden planner of some years ago, the late Percy Cane. In it, the roses are underplanted in the modern way with low-growing pinks, phlox and violas. Below the terrace walls are more borders; these are planted rather with shrubs such as philadelphus, buddleia and ceanothus than with herbaceous material, thus saving labour and providing height and form in winter.

The third of the terraces at Sutton Park is embellished with a lily pond. Water lilies star the surface, and a hundred gold fish show the glint of their scales between their shining pads.

Further afield than the three terraces that have been described are areas planted with rare trees, shading drifts of daffodils in spring, and here and there set with borders of shade-loving plants such as bergenias, hostas and Japanese anemones. Further to the east lies a wood with romantic paths cut through it and a fine central ride. This has for 'eye-catcher' a classical stone urn of great simplicity, placed at the junction of two woodland paths.

The garden at Sutton Park is not a garden on the scale of Hampton Court or Chatsworth. It is maintained to perfection by a minimum staff, and the hard physical work of its devoted owners. It is an example of how a handsome pleasure ground can still be well kept, if the owners are prepared to do much of the work themselves.

OPEN April 7th (approx) – September 29th (approx): Tuesday, Wednesday, Thursday and Sunday, 2 p.m. – 6 p.m. In October Sundays only (visitors should check before going).
LOCATION Entrance gates in village of Sutton on the Forest, about 8 miles north of York on the B1363.

ABOVE *A general view of the lay-out of the garden.*
Beyond lies a miniature park, with roundels of
trees in the Capability Brown manner.

4

SCOTLAND

EDZELL CASTLE, Angus
CRARAE, Argyllshire
TYNINGHAME, East Lothian
CRATHES CASTLE, Kincardineshire
INVEREWE, Ross-shire

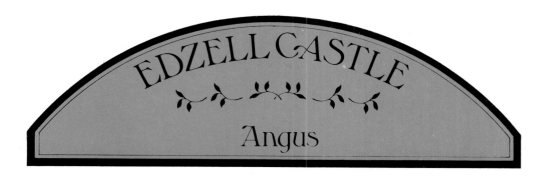

EDZELL CASTLE
Angus

It is not to Edzell Castle in Angus that the visitor comes in search of rare or tender plants. The interest and fascination of the garden does not lie in those. It is to be found in its architecture, its sophisticated layout, and in the fact that the garden or pleasance, now so beautifully restored, was first laid out all of three hundred and fifty years ago. The heraldic and symbolical carvings which embellish the garden at Edzell are surely unique in Scotland, and would be remarkable anywhere.

The late Professor Douglas Simpson, in his admirable guide book, tells us that the 'the Lichtsome Lindsays', a gifted, gallant, turbulent, gay and tragic race, remained in possession of Edzell until 1715, in which year, 'their affairs having fallen into hopeless embarrassment – the estates were sold....' The estate, castle and pleasance itself then fell on checkered days. The ravages of time, aided and abetted by King George's Hanoverian soldiery after the second Jacobite rebellion in 1745, and the bankruptcy of its new owners, took fearful toll. The castle's roof was stripped of its lead, the beech avenues were felled, and the pleasance itself became a wilderness. But its plan survived, and so did most of its unique sculptures. In 1932 the property came under the custody of HM Office of Works (now the Department of the Environment) who have carried out a masterly programme of repair and reconstruction.

Sir David Lindsay, the creator of the garden at Edzell, was a most unusual man for his time. He was widely travelled, a great scholar and the possessor of

RIGHT *A sculpture set in the wall, and dating from 1604, depicts the god Saturn holding a child by its leg. He had the unpleasant reputation of eating children. As the patron of cripples, he has one leg on a crutch.*

FAR RIGHT *A carved figure of Mars, in armour, with Aries, the Ram, at his feet.*

LEFT *Flowers are planted in some of the recesses in the walls.*

great taste. It was from Germany that he brought back the ideas for the extraordinary series of sculptures with which he decorated his garden. He died, as Professor Simpson tells us, 'in extraordinary debt – the penalty of his sumptuous tastes', but he left to Scotland, in his garden at Edzell, a legacy of the greatest value.

The garden is entered by two doors – one in the rose-red ruined walls of the castle itself, and one at the north end of the east wall. Over each door are identical heraldic stones, bearing the Lindsay arms, and their optimistic motto, '*Dum spiro spero*' ('While I breathe, I hope'). These stones are dated 1604.

'It is in the decorative treatment of the garden wall that Lord Edzell and his master mason have achieved their triumph.' And it is the garden wall, with its curiously carved niches, its sculptured panels, its snug nesting recesses, pediments and carved scrolls, which invites the closest study, always with Professor Simpson's guide book in hand.

On the east side the sculptures depict the planetary deities – a mailed figure with a shield for Jupiter, for instance, and a female figure 'with heart aflame' for Venus. On the south side are to be found carvings of the Liberal Arts – Grammar in a teacher's gown, Rhetoric, another female figure in full flood of declamation and Arithmetica 'doing a sum, and very perplexed thereby'.

On the west side there are sculptures symbolizing the cardinal virtues, with Faith bearing a much-damaged cross, Charity with a clutch of naked children, and Temperance diluting a wine cup with a jug of water.

Professor Simpson, in his notes, tells us:

Taken as a whole, the pleasance, with its sculptured wall and adjuncts, forms one of the most remarkable artistic monuments that Scotland can show. The significance of such a work cannot be understood unless it is considered in relation to its times . . . it is the enshrinement, in stone and lime, of a fleeting mood, never repeated in Scottish history. . . . Prior to the Union of Crowns (in 1603) such a work of art could scarcely have been conceived: with the outbreak of the wars of religion in 1637 an abrupt stop was put, for many a long day to come, to all such . . . cultural architectural efforts.

The garden at Edzell Castle is unique, and well repays connoisseurs of gardens who take the trouble to make their way there. Though remote, the garden lies off the main road between Aberdeen and Forfar and so is not difficult to find.

OPEN April – September: 9.30 a.m. – 7 p.m. (Sundays 2 p.m. – 7 p.m.): October – March, 9.30 a.m. – 4 p.m. (Sunday 2 p.m. – 4 p.m.).
LOCATION About 2 miles west of Edzell village, about 7 miles north of Brechin.

CRARAE
Argyllshire

The history of the great Scottish garden at Crarae dates from the first years of this century, when the Lady Campbell of the day, an aunt of that celebrated plantsman Reginald Farrer, whose *English Rock Garden* is one of the classics in garden literature, planted the first rarities in the garden. Many of her trees have now grown to forest size and present a splendid picture whether in their vivid spring leaf, brilliant autumn colour or, if they are evergreen, sculptured form all the year round.

The garden has been allowed to grow naturally, on the steep banks of a burn. The soil is acid, and perfect for the many rhododendrons for which Crarae has become famous.

Trees and shrubs from all over the world have been collected and brought to Crarae, as they have been to other gardens in Scotland and England with similar soils and as gentle climates; but at Crarae there seems to be evidence of a very special taste and knowledge in their arrangement. Sir George Campbell, father of the present owner, must have been in close communication with the feeling of the place, the differing plants being grouped so well and so naturally.

It might be asked what memories the visitor to Crarae carries away with him when he leaves. That must depend on whether he is the average garden visitor, delighted with the natural beauty of the garden-pictures which everywhere at Crarae meet his eye, or a horticulturally-minded expert.

LEFT *A rustic bridge crosses a glen, with tree-clad slopes on either side.*

A view of Crarae Lodge, which is set in a garden full of rare rhododendrons.
On the left is R. Goldsworth's yellow, campylocarpum caucasium, and the brilliant
Ivery's Scarlet, an early rhododendron hybrid.

Of the natural beauties, the long views through high groves of trees towards Loch Fyne will surely linger in the memory – as will the banks and slopes golden with primroses in spring, and misty with starred bluebells in early summer. The average garden visitor does not need to be a professional botanist to appreciate the brilliant sheet of colour presented by the massed azaleas on Flagstaff Hill, or to be astonished by the exotic size and shape of the gunneras, from Brazil, by the burnside. And he will certainly enquire about the scarlet-flowered embothriums from Chile, rare trees which were first grown in Britain in 1851 and are still unfamiliar to many.

But, as it has been said, 'to the botanist, to the real expert, Crarae offers endless treats' – Groves of young plants of Eucalyptus urnigera from Australia; the pale-flowered Hoheria Lyallii from New Zealand; and that great plant collector George Forrest's very own Rhododendron racemosum from China. Some of the treasures of the garden at Crarae are Pittosporum tenuifolium, 'whose size often astonishes visitors from New Zealand, its native heath', and a fine collection of williamsii camellias.

Crarae is a garden which amply rewards the thousands of visitors who come every year. But it is on so grand a scale that however many people throng it, it never seems crowded. It is surely one of the greatest and most naturally beautiful gardens in Scotland.

OPEN March 1st – October 31st: daily, 8 a.m. – 6 p.m.
LOCATION 1 mile from Minard on A83, midway between Inveraray and Lochgilphead.

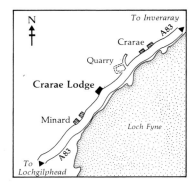

TYNINGHAME
East Lothian

Much of the garden at Tyninghame in East Lothian lies below the house itself – a fanciful castellated building of dark red sandstone. It is not a classically beautiful building, but it provides an almost fairytale background to the flowers. It could be the home of the Sleeping Beauty, or the palace of Prince Charming. The garden at Tyninghame is the creation of the present owners, Lord and Lady Haddington, and in its particularly special arrangement, would seem to be their very child, the immediate fruit of their imagination and fancy; almost an extension of their personality.

There was a garden at Tyninghame before the coming of the present Lord and Lady Haddington, but it was pompous, Victorian and possibly a trifle forbidding: there were stiff stone-edged flowerbeds, broad paths of gravel and acres of bleak lawns. There was little lightness, no fantasy, and we may be sure that the flower colours were those beloved by gardeners of a past generation – scarlet, yellow and an eye-searing blue. With the coming of the present Lady Haddington, a woman of enterprise, imagination and perfect taste, much was changed. Much, but not all. The garden was allowed to keep its Victorian plan, but pomposity was lightened and made attractive by deft planting. One part of the severe façade of the house was embellished with a light trellis-work screen clothed in roses, clematis and vines. The daunting expanses of gravel were enlivened with crisp white boxes, in the French style, and filled either with flowers or glossy bay trees. At the end of the long terrace, a raised Victorian seat of carved stone was given a setting of four cherry trees, the pyramidal Amanagawa which now stand behind it 'erect as footmen' and brighten the scene with their spring livery of pink blossom.

To the east of the house there lies the original Victorian parterre, replanted, when the writer last visited Tyninghame with roses, and the stark geometric pattern of its lay-out softened with plants of silver foliage. In the centre of this garden, which retains much of its original formality, is a tall sundial of a typically Scottish seventeenth-century design. It rewards close examination, with its elaborate set of dials and grotesque animals at its base.

Beyond this parterre lies a part of the garden which was only planted twenty-five years ago, and is very much in the modern taste. The planting was entirely the choice of Lady Haddington, and offers a good example of her gardening talent. It is on an informal plan, a series of beds set in turf, each one spilling over with flowers. In Lady Haddington's own words, it is 'stuffed with all the old roses . . . Tuscany, gallicas, Bourbons, damasks, and in addition, a few modern shrub roses like the old fashioned-looking Lavender Lassie, which has the same colouring and form as the old roses, to extend the flowering period'.

The fanciful roof-line of Tyninghame with white phlox, buddleias and grey cushions of Santolina incana.

Among the old roses grow silver-leaved plants – artemisias, Senecio greyii, santolina (cotton lavender), ordinary lavender (no relation to the previously mentioned cotton variety) and that fine salvia which one so seldom sees but which is such an excellent plant, Salvia turkestanica, with silver-haired leaves and bracts of pale mauve flowers. The visitor to Tyninghame leaves this charming little garden by an iron gate: on either side are brick piers bearing Italian statues of smiling children.

A walk, between tall trees and lavish plantings of rhododendrons and azaleas, leads to the old walled garden, nearly a quarter of a mile away. This is set out in the old Scottish fashion, with wide turf paths, neatly shorn hedges, and flowerbeds edged with box. As centre point there is a fountain, with water falling from horses' heads.

From this enclosed garden, a gate with keystone dated 1666 leads to one of the sights of Tyninghame – an apple tunnel, a hundred yards long, and all of eighty years old. At one end there is a graceful statue of Flora, and at the other, one of Ganymede, cup-bearer to the gods in classical times.

A wide gravel terrace might seem daunting without 'its crisp white boxes in the French style'. In the distance four slender Prunus serrulata Amanagawa.

A petal-strewn path under a canopy of roses.

On his return to the house, the visitor sees another part of the garden which has been completely transformed, though still keeping its original Victorian lay-out. This consists of a lawn, with raised flowerbeds contained in grey-stone walls and low buttresses. These heavy Victorian embellishments (they were placed in the garden in 1828) 'have been enlivened by a typical example of Lady Haddington's fancy, and are now crowned with pyramids of wood, over which are trained yellow roses and clematis, and underplanted with purple sage and dark red Rhus cotinus', the point of this particular planting being to blend with and complement the reddish-pink walls of the house. Treated in such an imaginative way, the rather clumsy stone-edged beds make garden features which are both practical and decorative.

Before leaving, the visitor to Tyninghame must inspect the garden which is Lord Haddington's special care – the Heath Garden. Heath gardens look specially well in Scotland (better than they do in the south) and the one at Tyninghame seems particularly suitable for its site, with the pepperpot turrets of the house showing over the pink, mauve, grey and sea-green colouring of the massed ericas. Heath gardens supply colour for many months of the year, and the weed-suppressing qualities of ericas is unsurpassed – two factors of great importance in gardening today.

The garden at Tyninghame is half an hour's walk, over springing turf, from the shores of the Firth of Forth. Across the Firth lies the misty shore of Fife. Nearer, in the land and sea-scape, looms the primeval shape of the Bass Rock, wreathed with a constant cloud of sea gulls.

It is the sea which makes the winters at Tyninghame as gentle as they are, encouraging the garden to flower and flourish in the way it does. It is a garden which offers the visitor many, and very special pleasures.

OPEN May 1st – September 30th: Monday, Tuesday, Wednesday, Thursday, and Friday, 1.30 p.m. – 4.30 p.m. (No dogs allowed.)
LOCATION Take A1 from Haddington towards Dunbar. Turn left to East Linton, then take B1047 to Tyninghame village.

CRATHES CASTLE
Kincardineshire

The short reign of Mary, Queen of Scots, (1561–7) was too troublous a time for building, yet during those few years one castle at least was built in Scotland by the ancient family of Burnett. It has been occupied by them ever since, and the first-time visitor to the garden at Crathes cannot fail to be impressed by the romantic silhouette of their Castle, standing high over the rushing waters of the River Dee.

Its outline comprises all the architectural fancies that one expects in Scottish baronial architecture: grey-stone turrets, craw-stepped gables, machicolations, bartizans and elaborate corbelling. But the architectural fantasies of Crathes Castle are genuine and of the sixteenth century; they are not, as is often the case with buildings in Scottish baronial style, the heavy-handed imitations of Victorian architects.

Over the turbulent years of Scottish history the fabric of Crathes Castle had suffered little, until some years ago when a fire did serious damage to the Queen Anne Wing. In spite of that, it is still one of the most fascinating castles of Scotland to visit, and is open to the public for many months in the year. And it has a garden which is worthy of it. This is one of the earliest of formal gardens in Scotland, and was already celebrated in 1714, when Sir Samuel Forbes wrote, 'The House of Crathes is well built . . . the gardens produce delicate fruit: the soil is warm: the victual substantious and weighty.' At that time the yew hedges, now such a magnificent feature of the garden at Crathes, were already twelve years old, having been planted in the year of Queen Anne's accession in 1702. These hedges make the divisions between some of the

LEFT *Crathes Castle was built in the short troubled reign of Mary Queen of Scots (1561–7). It is set in a very beautiful and romantic garden.*

BELOW *The overall colour scheme of the Fountain Garden at Crathes is blue.*

several smaller gardens which go to make up the intriguing pattern of the garden as a whole. For the entire complex is divided up, very much in the taste of today, into a series of plots, each with its own name, its own colour scheme, and its own character. Seen from an upstairs window, these separate gardens look like an elaborate carpet, lapping the castle walls, and merging imperceptibly into the surrounding landscape of Kincardine.

The garden at Crathes shelters a most remarkable collection of plants, and the visitor should visit the various enclosures one by one, and examine carefully the interesting specimens they contain. First, the Pool Garden, under the castle's very walls. Here, early on in his tour, the visitor finds much to make him exclaim: the white-flowered Styrax hemsleyana from China, for instance, and the rare Buddleia Colvilei, with its hanging racemes of pink flowers, which grows only in the most favoured gardens in the south. Nearby are a fine specimen of the New Zealand lace-bark (Hoheria populneis) which shows saucer-sized

Well-tailored topiary and hedges make the bold pattern of the garden.

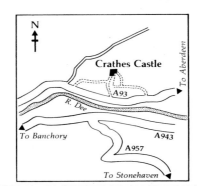

Brightly coloured herbaceous borders seen from under the silvery branches and bole of a mature eucalyptus Gunnii.

flowers in late summer, and two quite outstanding honeysuckles, the Chinese Lonicera tragophylla with long yellow trumpets, and one of the most beautiful of them all, Lonicera splendida, with silvery leaves and champagne-coloured flowers. The latter comes from Spain, the home of Don da Silva Feijoa who gave his name to another unusual plant at Crathes, Feijoa sellowiana. This is described in the Royal Horticultural Society's *Dictionary of Gardening* as 'not quite hardy in our average climate', so that it is a tribute to the gardening skill of the owners of Crathes to find it growing there in the open, in a Scottish county which derives no benefit from the Gulf Stream, and which in fact lies open to all the chilling gales which sweep over Kincardine from the east coast . . . a far cry from Uruguay, which is feijoa's country of origin.

In the Fountain Garden there are mostly blue flowers: blue annuals growing round the fountain, and, presiding, a magnificent Paulownia imperialis with blue foxglove flowers borne in very early spring. These are all too often marred

173

*A picture which gives a good idea of the standard of maintenance which makes
the garden at Crathes so unique: the Colour Garden.*

by frost, but make it a wonderful sight when the weather has been kind. Not far away grows another shrub which comes into its own later in the year, Cercidiphyllum japonicum, a medium-sized shrub which puts up a brilliant firework display of colour in autumn.

When the writer of this book visited Crathes the apple trees were hung with fruit and the Rose Garden was as brave a sight as the rose garden at Haddon, shown elsewhere in these pages. As at Haddon, the Rose Garden at Crathes was also largely planted with floribunda roses, tellingly interplanted with the white, bell-flowered giant summer hyacinth (Galtonia candicans), and drifts of the annual red orach (Atriplex hortensis), a decorative kind of spinach. This is a most effective and practical planting combination. Once planted, galtonias can be left undisturbed for years; while the red spinach seeds itself generously every year – a good example of gardening skill and imagination. Nearby grew a good specimen of Davidia involucrata, or dove tree, which covers its branches every spring with white leaf-bracts round the inconspicuous flowers. These look for all the world like fluttering doves. It is also, less romantically, called the handkerchief tree.

In another warm corner, in the Aviary Border, the Chilean gazania (Mutisia oligodon) flowers in autumn. This is a rare plant indeed, with a striking climbing habit, and pink daisy flowers.

In one of the Four Squares, as four of the enclosed gardens at Crathes are called, the writer particularly noticed some brilliant tigridias whose exotic flowers last only one day, but follow each other in bright succession all through the summer, while in the Trough and Doocot Gardens grew day lilies, peonies, autumn crocus and those giant lilies from the Himalayas, Lilium giganteum.

To conclude these notes, let us quote what a great connoisseur of gardens – and owner of Great Dixter – Mr Christopher Lloyd, had to say about the garden at Crathes.

It is not only stuffed with interesting and beautiful plants which one is amazed to see flourishing in this least hospitable corner of the British Isles, but it is extremely well laid out and is planted according to the kind of plan that I should never be strong-minded enough to adopt myself without starting again from scratch. A fascinating border, for instance, devoted to foliage plants; a double herbaceous border entirely concentrated on a staggering display of herbaceous plants for June effect and another most subtly conceived garden where purple flowers and foliage are contrasted with pale yellows and lime greens.

Throughout this much praised garden at Crathes there runs a theme which is noticeable as one passes from enclosure to enclosure: it is hard to define, difficult to identify, but as each border is examined and the peaceful atmosphere absorbed, the visitor realizes that here is a garden which owes everything, not to its historic frame, certainly not to the amiability of the climate, but to the taste, science and gardening skill of the owners who have planted the garden and dressed its borders so well.

OPEN All year round, daily from 9.30 a.m.
LOCATION 3 miles from Banchory on A93.

*The white house of Inverewe with a mixed border of herbaceous
plants, set, as they always should be, in bold groups.*

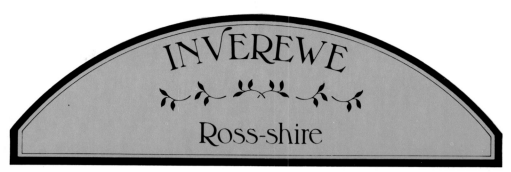

INVEREWE
Ross-shire

It can be said with confidence that Scotland was anything but bonny three hundred and fifty years ago. The heather and the mountains were there, it is true, but there were few trees, few flowers, and, in a country which was continually at war either with England or itself, very few gardens. The old prehistoric forests had been cut down for fuel, what flowers there existed were wild, and houses were either fortresses or hovels. The climate, too, had a strange reputation. Few plants, apparently, could survive it, and those that could were freakish, to say the least. Aenaeas Piccolomini, afterwards Pope Pius II, who toured Scotland in the reign of James I, mentions a pear bush which produced fruit in the form of geese, which dropped off and flew away. He also noted the complete lack of trees and general bleakness of the countryside. Nor were vegetables cultivated to any extent; the Scots in general did not like them, and laughed at the Grant clan who did – 'the soft Kail-eating Grants'. The reputation of Scotland's climate was discouraging, and in the seventeenth century Fynes Morison wrote: 'In the northerne parts of England they have small pleasantnesse . . . or abundance of fruit and flowers, so in Scotland they must have lesse, or none at all.' Even Dr Johnson who, admittedly, was against Scotland generally, described the climate as so bad that the Scots had to grow barley under glass.

How wrong they all were. Scotland has just as good a gardening climate as England, and in parts better. It is fundamentally incorrect to think that the farther north you are, the fewer plants you can grow. A truer line to take is the west–east one: the Atlantic-washed coast of both England and Scotland has a far milder climate than the east coast. There are few plants growing in the south of England which cannot be even better grown on the favoured west coast of Scotland, and it is here that the beautiful garden at Inverewe is situated. The success of the garden is due not only to the benefit of the Gulf Stream but also to the grandeur of the garden's setting, and to the way in which the garden has been allowed to grow naturally. The collection of rare and delicate plants that it contains is second to none in Britain.

The garden was first cultivated over 110 years ago, when Osgood Mackenzie, Laird of Gairloch, bought the property. At that time there was hardly any pleasure ground and 'no trees or shrubs in sight, except one tiny bush of dwarf willow about three feet high. This was preserved in the garden for many years but has now gone.'

The Inverewe peninsula was not an obvious choice for a garden. Its Gaelic name was Am Ploc Ard – the 'High Lump', and the ground was a mass of Torridonian sandstone. It was quite bare of vegetation except for some stunted

heather and straggling Crowberry (Empetrum nigrum). What soil there was was rough black peat; acid, but not deep. Much had been carted away for fuel by the crofters. There was hardly any good soil at all: little gravel or sand. In places there was 'a jumble of rotten rock. One redeeming feature . . . was that the rock was not solid, but broke up easily, and in places showed veins of soft pink clay.' Even so, when the garden was first planted, good soil had to be carried in in baskets.

The peninsula in those days was swept by Atlantic winds, for except for the low hills of the Isle of Lewis, forty miles out to sea, there is nothing between Inverewe and the coast of Labrador. Or at least there was nothing until Osgood Mackenzie planted the necessary windbreaks. The terrain caught every gale that blew, and was drenched regularly with sea-spray. However there was the Gulf Stream, with the benefits it brings; and as soon as the future garden was protected by a deer and rabbit fence, as well as the all-important windbreaks, it began to prosper. The shelter-belts were of Corsican pine and Scots fir, Rhododendron ponticum, Douglas fir and many other conifers. Where the soil was deep enough a few specimens of Sequoia gigantea were planted – the giant wellingtonia, sometimes, unhappily, referred to as sequoiadendron.

Soon it was considered safe to set rarer, less tough trees, and eucalyptus and the more delicate rhododendrons took their place in the garden. Today all Osgood Mackenzie's trees have grown amazingly and are twined about with uncommon creepers from all over the world. Climbing plants such as the Tasmanian Billardiera longiflora with its striking blue berries, the coral plant (Berberidopsis corallina) from Chile, and the South American glory flower (Eccromocarpus scaber), with orange-coloured trumpet flowers.

One point about the garden which the observant visitor will quickly appreciate is the particular beauty of the silver birches (Betula pendula), especially when they are growing near rhododendrons. For only trees with bark of un-sullied silver are allowed to establish themselves at Inverewe, and any with too much black on their bark are ruthlessly eliminated. The contrast of the silver against the dark green of the rhododendrons' foliage is spectacular. Another notable feature is the red Torridonian sandstone, which, pushing up through the ground here and there throughout the garden, makes a pleasing setting for flowering shrubs and small trees.

There is an excellent guide book to the garden at Inverewe, from which many of the facts in these notes have been taken. With it in hand, the visitor can pass from one part of the garden to another and learn exactly what plants to look for in each particular section – and some of the different sections of the garden have the most endearing names. One is known as Japan, because of a double pink cherry which once grew in it; here most of the trees are evergreen, so that it is a part of the garden which looks as well in winter as it does in summer. Another section of the garden is called Creag A Lios – a natural rock garden, surrounded by rare rhododendrons, and with plants showing their colour against a background of the local sandstone. Yet another part of this treasure garden of plants is an enclosure named, whimsically, Bambooselem, where, protected by thick plantings of bamboos, many rare plants flourish – among them the Chilean Guevina avellana, two fine hoherias from New Zealand, and a good specimen of Davidia involucrata, the dove, or more prosaically, handkerchief tree. It is perhaps in Bambooselem that the finest of all the trees

LEFT *A view, over flowering brooms, towards an inlet of the sea.*

BELOW *Meconopsis betonicifolia, the Blue Poppy from Tibet, must have a cool root-run and acid soil. Until recently it was known as M. Baileyi, after its discoverer in 1924, Captain F. M. Bailey.*

of Inverewe is to be found, a fifty-year-old Magnolia Campbellii, which shows its spectacular pink flowers in late March.

One last plant out of hundreds must be admired. Myosotidium hortensia, the Chatham Island forget-me-not. This is a very rare plant indeed, and not an easy one to grow, unless it is given the curious fertiliser it prefers – seaweed and dead fish. With this unappetising diet it will flourish, and myosotidium, with its handsome ribbed leaves and hydrangea-like heads of flower, is now well established at Inverewe.

The admirable guide book to the garden ends with a paragraph headed 'When is the best time to visit Inverewe?' and goes on to say that the question is a difficult one to answer as conditions vary from year to year – though there is always much of interest in the garden and at no time is it quite without flower of some kind.

A famous horticulturist once visited Inverewe, and the owner, feeling rather shy at letting him see the garden, apologised for its unkempt appearance: 'I knew he had about fifty gardeners, while I had only two and a half! However, after a tour of inspection the famous man's parting words were, "Don't alter it, it is lovely. It reminds me of some wild corner in Burma or Northern China".'

ABOVE *'Don't alter it, it's lovely'* *(see text).*

RIGHT *View towards the sea, with an azalea in the foreground.*

OPEN Daily, all year round, from dawn to dusk.
LOCATION Near Poolewe on A832 between Gairloch and Aultbea.

USEFUL PUBLICATIONS

Anyone interested in visiting gardens should acquire the following three very useful publications which give details and dates of hundreds of private gardens which are open to the public only on certain days in aid of different charities:

The National Gardens Scheme Yellow Book, 57 Lower Belgrave Street, London SW1 (40p approx).

Gardeners' Sunday booklet *Gardens to Visit,* Gardeners' Sunday Organization, White Witches, Claygate Road, Dorking, Surrey (30p approx).

Scotland's Gardens Scheme booklet, Scotland's Gardens Scheme, 26 Castle Terrace, Edinburgh (30p approx).

ACKNOWLEDGMENTS

The photographs in this book were taken by the author. Additional material was supplied by the following, to whom grateful thanks are extended:

John Bethell: 44(2), 45, 101, 103, endpapers
British Tourist Authority: 106, 113, 114, 116
Dr J. G. Burgess: 157(2), 158, 159
Alex. Lawrie Factors Ltd (Beric Tempest): 95, 96, 97
K. Lemmon: 156
National Trust: 32, 34, 40(2), 66, 67(below), 82(below), 83, 84, 85, 86, 102
National Trust for Scotland: 158–9 (Woodmansterne), 171 (Woodmansterne), 172, 173 (Woodmansterne), 174–5 (Woodmansterne), 176–7, 178, 179, 180, 181
Harry Smith (J. E. Downward copyright): 52, 56–7
Alton Towers: 140, 141, 142, 143
Marshall Cavendish Picture Library (Photo. C. Watmough): 1

Illustrations on section openings

Pages 10–11: Flowering rhododendrons at Exbury.
Pages 68–9: A pot of fuchsias at Powis Castle.
Pages 104–5: The house at Newby Hall.
Pages 158–9: Crathes Castle from the Lower Garden.